THE RESTRICTION OF NATIONAL SOVEREIGNTY

Scholarly Articles by Peter Fritz Walter

The Law of Evidence

The Restriction of National Sovereignty

Alternative Medicine and Wellness Techniques

Consciousness and Shamanism

Creative Prayer

Soul Jazz

The Ego Matter

The Star Script

The Lunar Bull

Basics of Mythology

Basics of Feng Shui

Power or Depression?

The Mythology of Narcissism

Normative Psychoanalysis

Notes on Consciousness

Patterns of Perception

Sane Child vs. Insane Society

Basics of the Science of Mind

The Secret Science

Oedipal Hero

Processed Reality

THE RESTRICTION OF NATIONAL SOVEREIGNTY

BASICS FOR LAW SCHOOL

BY PETER FRITZ WALTER

Published by Sirius-C Media Galaxy LLC

113 Barksdale Professional Center, Newark, Delaware, USA

©2015 Peter Fritz Walter. Some rights reserved.

2017 Revised, Updated and Reformatted Edition.

Creative Commons Attribution 4.0 International License

This publication may be distributed, used for an adaptation or for derivative works, also for commercial purposes, as long as the rights of the author are attributed. The attribution must be given to the best of the user's ability with the information available. Third party licenses or copyright of quoted resources are untouched by this license and remain under their own license.

The moral right of the author has been asserted

Set in Palatino

Designed by Peter Fritz Walter

ISBN 978-1-515184-48-5

Scholarly Articles, Vol. 2

Publishing Categories
Law / International

Publisher Contact Information
publisher@sirius-c-publishing.com
http://sirius-c-publishing.com

Author Contact Information
pfw@peterfritzwalter.com

About Dr. Peter Fritz Walter
http://peterfritzwalter.com

About the Author

Parallel to an international law career in Germany, Switzerland and the United States, Dr. Peter Fritz Walter (Pierre) focused upon fine art, cookery, astrology, musical performance, social sciences and humanities.

He started writing essays as an adolescent and received a high school award for creative writing and editorial work for the school magazine.

After finalizing his law diplomas, he graduated with an LL.M. in European Integration at Saarland University, Germany, in 1982, and with a Doctor of Law title from University of Geneva, Switzerland, in 1987.

He then took courses in psychology at the University of Geneva and interviewed a number of psychotherapists in Lausanne and Geneva, Switzerland. His interest was intensified through a hypnotherapy with an Ericksonian American hypnotherapist in Lausanne. This led him to the recovery and healing of his inner child.

After a second career as a corporate trainer and personal coach, Pierre retired in 2004 as a full-time writer, philosopher and consultant.

His nonfiction books emphasize a systemic, holistic, cross-cultural and interdisciplinary perspective, while his fiction works and short stories focus upon education, philosophy, perennial wisdom, and the poetic formulation of an integrative worldview.

Pierre is a German-French bilingual native speaker and writes English as his 4th language after German, Latin and French. He also reads source literature for his research works in Spanish, Italian, Portuguese, and Dutch. In addition, Pierre has notions of Thai, Khmer, Chinese, Japanese, and Vietnamese.

All of Pierre's books are hand-crafted and self-published, designed by the author. Pierre publishes via his Delaware company, Sirius-C Media Galaxy LLC, and under the imprints of IPUBLICA and SCM (Sirius-C Media).

Nationalism, the patriotic spirit, class and race consciousness, are all ways of the self, and therefore separative. After all, what is a nation but a group of individuals living together for economic and self-protective reasons? Out of fear and acquisitive self-defense arises the idea of my country, with its boundaries and tariff walls, rendering brotherhood and the unity of man impossible.

—J. Krishnamurti, Education and the Significance of Life (1978)

There exists perhaps no conception the meaning of which is more controversial than that of sovereignty. It is an indisputable fact that this conception, from the moment when it was introduced into political science until the present day, has never had a meaning which was universally agreed upon.

—Lassa Oppenheim, International Law (1928)

The author's profits from this book are being donated to charity.

Contents

Introduction 9
What is National Sovereignty?

Chapter One 17
The Rise of National Sovereignty

Chapter Two 35
The Restriction of National Sovereignty
Introduction	35
State Trading	41
The Restrictive Immunity Concept and the Burden of Proof	50
Immunity from Jurisdiction	59
Immunity from Execution	63
The Signal Function of Restricted Sovereignty	67

Chapter Three 75
The Empowered Citizen
An Important Meeting	75
The World Model Revisited	78
A Changing Social Framework	89
An Uncanny International Organization	94

Chapter Four 111
The United States of Europe
Introduction	111
The Plans for 'Eternal Peace'	120

Abbé de Saint-Pierre	126
Jean-Jacques Rousseau	128
Immanuel Kant	133
Saint-Simon	139
Coudenhove-Kalergi	148
INTEGRATION VS. CONSTITUTION	151
The Integrational Model	154
The Constitutional Model	159
A EUROPEAN CONSTITUTION?	161

BIBLIOGRAPHY 177
Contextual Bibliography

PERSONAL NOTES 187

Introduction

What is National Sovereignty?

Sovereignty is a concept that describes the *scope of power of rulers, sovereigns, heads of state or governments*; it came upon us from the Romans who expressed it as the idea that the Emperor exercised an absolute reign; the same idea reigned in old Egypt where the Pharaoh had absolute power over the land and the people.

The ancient peoples did not yet talk about *sovereignty* in the conceptual sense we know it, but the idea was basically the same.

It has to be seen that the monarchs of the feudal aristocracy during the Middle-Ages

THE RESTRICTION OF NATIONAL SOVEREIGNTY

were not sovereigns in that quality as their rulership was limited, and not absolute.

The feudal system however was rather the exception, while absolute sovereignty was later established as the rule in international law. There was nonetheless a continuity in the basic concept of sovereignty, while its scope and its possible limits were a matter of scholarly debate, from the time of the Romans through to the present day.

This is how the concept changed in its definition, scope, and application, until a certain uniformity and consensus was reached during the *Age of Enlightenment*.

The current notion of state sovereignty was laid down in the *Treaty of Westphalia (1648)*, which marked the end of the *Thirty Years War (1618-1648)* and which, in relation to states, codified the *basic principles of territorial integrity, border inviolability, and supremacy of the state,* as opposed to the authority of the Church. It was from that time also that international law described a sovereign is a supreme lawmaking authority.

After the centuries of the abusive regime of the Church, with all their witchhunts and the holocaust perpetrated by the Inquisition in Europe, sovereignty reemerged as a concept in the late 1500s, a time when civil wars had created a craving for stronger central authority, when monarchs had begun to gather power into their own hands at the expense of the nobility, and the modern nation state was emerging.

Jean Bodin and Thomas Hobbes presented theories of sovereignty calling for strong central authority in the form of absolute monarchy.

In his treatise *On Sovereignty (1576/2009),* Jean Bodin argued that it is inherent in the

THE RESTRICTION OF NATIONAL SOVEREIGNTY

nature of the state that sovereignty is *absolute* and *perpetual*. This modern conceptualization of sovereignty later led to what is called *absolutism*, and what became the leading version of rulership for the French kings. In fact, the strange thing is that when the Church began to lose its absolute power in Europe, the sovereign power of the monarch was defined with religious overtones.

Bodin and other scholars wrote that the doctrine of sovereignty is conferred by divine law; this is how the idea came up that kings enjoyed some form of *divine right*.

Thomas Hobbes, in his book *Leviathan (1651/2006)*, introduced an early version of the *social contract*, a theory later taken up and developed by Jean-Jacques Rousseau (1712-1778). Hobbes deduced from the definition of sovereignty that it must be *absolute* and *indivisible*. The idea that the ruler's sovereignty is in effect conferred to him by the people in return for his maintaining their safety, led him to conclude that if the ruler fails to do this, the people are released from their obligation to obey him, which can as a hypothesis be seen verified later on with the *French Revolution (1789-1799)*.

Niccolò Machiavelli, Thomas Hobbes, John Locke, and Montesquieu are key figures in the unfolding of the concept of sovereignty.

The second book of Rousseau's *Social Contract (1762/1997)* deals with sovereignty and its rights. Sovereignty, or the general will, is inalienable according to Rousseau, for the will cannot be transmitted; it is indivisible, since it is essentially general; it is infallible and always right, determined and limited in its power by the common interest; it acts through laws. In the third book, however, he argued critically that 'the growth of the state will give the trustees of public authority more and means to abuse their power,' which is exactly what was going to be seen on the political arena later on. And here we can see one of the reasons why the French Revolution shifted the possession of sovereignty from the sovereign ruler to the nation and its people.

West's Encyclopedia of American Law (2008) defines sovereignty as 'the supreme, absolute, and uncontrollable power by which an independent state is governed and from which all specific political powers are derived; the intentional independence of a state, combined with the right and power of regulating its internal affairs without foreign interference'.

Sovereignty is thus the power of a state to do everything necessary to govern itself, such as making, executing, and applying laws, imposing and collecting taxes, making war and peace and forming treaties or engaging in commerce with foreign nations.

The individual States of the United States do not possess the powers of external sovereignty, such as the right to deport undesirable persons, but each does have certain attributes of internal sovereignty, such as the power to regulate the acquisition and transfer of property within its borders. The sovereignty of a State is determined with reference to the U.S. Constitution, which is 'the supreme law of the land.'

Chapter One

The Rise of National Sovereignty

The single most important leverage for world peace is the *restriction of national sovereignty* to a residual concept, transferring the ensuing sovereignty power vacuum to an *international organism* that shall be competent for matters of 'world government,' as for example the peaceful settlement of conflicts, international currency management, ecological sanity requirements for businesses and related conflict solution, international arbitrage services, as well as strategic, economic or humanitarian help for developing countries, and last not least survival support for ethnic, racial or otherwise

THE RESTRICTION OF NATIONAL SOVEREIGNTY

endangered minorities and tribal cultures wherever located, within any of the nation states.

With the transfer of national sovereignty to a supranational authority, the nation states party of such an international agreement, that forms the constitutional charter of the authority to be created, would transfer all competencies for handling the above-mentioned international affairs to that organism called 'World Government' or otherwise.

The idea is not new, as I will demonstrate below, where I report some of the well-known *Plans for Eternal Peace in Europe*, as they were brought up by great philosophers such as Immanuel Kant, Jean-Jacques Rousseau, and others.

Interestingly enough, from the many thinkable solutions for establishing world peace, these plans all converged to a single monolithic idea, which is the *restriction of national sovereignty*; it is interesting because when the first of these ideas emerged, in the 17th century, the nation state itself was still in the cradle; it was around that time that the very notion of the nation state was beginning to emerge in international law.

Before that time, the 'state' was notably not yet a political and legal entity as in the craftsmen-society, a concept of 'national power' was not yet existent; power structures at that time were by and large *regional*, and it was through inbreeding, that is the fusion of large nobility blood lines, that this regional power structure gradually expanded into the later nation states. But with that to happen, there was at the same time an inherent danger to the peace of that ancient society; the danger was that the cross-breeding structure within the European nobility that was *actually interlinking the old world*, was breaking apart because of the artificial construct of 'national sovereignty.' Thus, as most international law scholars agree, with the abandonment of that kind of flexible 'networked' nobility structure of the princedoms and kingdoms developing into a rigid scheme of nations who, through the very idea of national sovereignty, were fundamentally hostile to each other, the soil for all wars and civil wars to occur later in history was prepared.

It is national sovereignty, as an idea, which by the way is not something rooted in history, but a construct that was prepared in most of its contours by *Count Niccoló Machiavelli*, that was the single most explosive political concept in human history, leading to rampant political violence and tyranny, and endless wars and civil wars culminating in the two World Wars, in the 20th century.

> —See Niccoló Machiavelli, The Prince, New York, Soho Books, 2009. Written in 1513.

What I am saying here is not an insight that can only be gained now, in the 21st century, but a fact that already some brilliant contemporaries of Machiavelli identified, which is why they were alarmed about 'the state of the world' and came up with peace plans, some of which were denominated as 'urgency solutions' for preventing immanent war.

Alvin Toffler writes in his book *The Third Wave (1984)*, in a chapter entitled 'A Frenzy of Nations:'

> Starting with the American and French revolutions and continuing through the nineteenth century, a *frenzy of nationalism* swept across the industrializing parts of the world. Germany's three hundred and fifty petty, diverse, quarreling mini-states needed to be

THE RESTRICTION OF NATIONAL SOVEREIGNTY

> combined into a single national market—das Vaterland. Italy—broken into pieces and ruled variously by the House of Savoy, the Vatican, the Austrian Habsburgs, and the Spanish Bourbons—had to be united. Hungarians, Serbs, Croats, Frenchmen, and others all suddenly developed mystical affinities for their fellows. Poets exalted the national spirit. Historians discovered long-lost heroes, literature, and folklore. Composers wrote hymns to nationhood. *All at precisely the moment when industrialization made it necessary. (Id., 81, emphasis mine)*

I found Toffler's books only after finalizing this study, and to my surprise I note a similar line of reasoning. In my scholarly article *Natural Order (2015)*, I am discussing the entire human evolution as a process that went over three basic phases, *thesis, antithesis* and *synthesis*. And with Toffler I find the same kind of reasoning expressed as a concept of *three waves*, the *First Wave*, which I called thesis or original order, the *Second Wave*, which I call antithesis or the disturbed or industrial order and the *Third Wave*, synthesis, which could be called the new order. Toffler pursues on the subject of nationalism:

> What one saw, therefore, in one country after another, was the rise of this powerful new entity – the nation. In this way the world map came to be divided into a set of neat, nonoverlapping patches of red, pink, orange, yellow, or green, *and the nation-state system became one of the key structures of Second Wave civilization. (Id., 83, emphasis mine)*

The following quote stands symbolic for the injustice and immense cruelty and power of the antithesis over the natural order, and explains in a metaphorical manner the chaos it created in the world to this very day:

> In reality, negotiations between *Second Wave* merchants and *First Wave* people over sugar, copper, cocoa, or other resources were often totally lopsided.
>
> On one side of the table sat money-shrewd European or American traders backed by huge companies, extensive banking networks, powerful technologies, and strong national governments. On the other one might find a local lord or tribal chieftain whose people had scarcely entered the money system and whose

THE RESTRICTION OF NATIONAL SOVEREIGNTY

> economy was based on small-scale agriculture or village crafts. On one side sat the agents of a thrusting, alien, mechanically advanced civilization, convinced of its own superiority and ready to use bayonets or machine guns to prove it. On the other sat representatives of small prenational tribes or principalities, armed with arrows and spears. (Id., 87)

We are today in a completely different world. While we still have national governments, national identities and national budgets, and while we still have borders and passport controls, the world has considerably changed since the 17th century. It's virtually no more the same world. We are all interconnected today through not only the electronic wires, the Internet, and wireless communication, handphones, and satellites, and worldwide publicity, but we are also having the knowledge now, through quantum physics and other cutting-edge sciences that we are *not alone and separate* as human beings, but interlinked through the quantum field, the underlying matrix of all life in the universe.

Today, the worldwide structural shifts in the economies, and the gradual formation of what could be called a global network economy force all of us to change and adapt our businesses and personal paradigms to globalization. They force us to look at life in an entirely different way.

These global structural changes already now, but more still in the decades to come, will incite many traditional businesses to renew themselves in a way to being more flexible, more 'movable' and more unconventional for implementing new and integrated solutions.

Economies are likely to crash if they are unable to do the structural changes that globalization requires.

THE RESTRICTION OF NATIONAL SOVEREIGNTY

New ways for financing projects of global dimensions will be found.

Today, not only economists begin to doubt if the world economy is going to be maintained on the sole basis of a paper currency such as the dollar; there will probably be a pool of prime currencies that compose, and safeguard, the 'world currency' of the future.

This process of working out something like a 'world currency pool' is likely to take a *leveraging function* in the paradigm change from sovereign nations to a world government where every nation joins in with all their cultural, ethnic and social diversity, but with a shared restricted sovereignty that would relegate world wars to the past.

The concept of sovereignty, today, cannot be seen in the ways Bodin, Hobbes or Rousseau saw it back in the *Age of*

THE RISE OF NATIONAL SOVEREIGNTY

Enlightenment. These times are definitely gone.

The world consists today of about *two hundred sovereign nation states,* while at the time it was a handful European hegemonies who were controlling the rest of the world.

This gives a totally different picture, and also a different power picture. When powers are differently aligned, sovereignty is relativized, and therefore must be redefined, because sovereignty is power, nothing but power, if one sees that power given by god, by the people or by a parliament doesn't make a difference.

And when we speak about power, we also speak about the power of the individual, which today surely is greater than back in the times of absolutism.

THE RESTRICTION OF NATIONAL SOVEREIGNTY

In addition, an organization such as the Christian Church that through their power games manipulated and infantilized the masses in the whole of Europe is unthinkable today.

Another factor of change is the information flow that today assumed such gigantic proportions that only professional media experts can channel it and provide daily information that is even remotely accurate.

While abuses still occur, and while conflict and wars still are daily reality, the difference is that today every single human on the globe can instantly be informed about them, and can make up their mind about them.

This power of information has rarely ever been validated in international law textbooks, as international law scholars often are living in ivory towers, which is why their political predictions, if ever they engage in them, are to be taken with a grain of salt.

It is different, as a general rule, with *international lawyers* who have seen how law and custom get embroiled in, for example, sovereign immunity litigation, and who know that the often lauded precision of international law is largely a myth.

Today, with the rise of the international consumer culture, while there are of course new pitfalls for state power crushing the individual through a blown-up control and supervision machinery, there is potentially and despite all a higher chance for the individual to emerge more powerful than this ever was thinkable in the past. This fact has in my view not yet been validated in international law textbooks, as it's perhaps of a mere psychological nature for the moment, until it will be solidified by paradigm changes and legal reform in the future.

In the years to come, the rising political transparence and the fact that power abuses are relatively quickly unveiled and revealed to the public, will gradually disempower the worldwide truth-holder conglomerates and emasculate their imperialistic monopolies and favoritism that enriches an oligarchy beyond all measure, while leaving hundreds of millions mentally, materially and spiritually impoverished!

On the other hand, new global business opportunities will arise for those who build on freedom and democracy and who listen to the true needs of the masses. While companies that build on privileges or outmoded traditions, or else a blown-up self-image, or that adhere to undemocratic or even tyrannical forms of leadership will be surprised how quickly and effectively the new era will literally wipe them from the surface of international business.

The highest reward will be for those who serve the customer and who build a service-oriented business model that empowers the consumer, that is transparent, that gives options and that is consistent in structure and constant in time.

In this sense, I see consumer culture, with its *network structure* and global scope, as a potentially fertile soil for sovereignty going global in the sense of being transformed into a concept of 'sovereign participation' in a world government that represents the interests of *all humans on the globe*, whatever their cultural, religious, ethnic or social belonging.

I do not dare a prognosis how what Alvin Toffler called *Powershift* will make its way through humanity and how big the damage will be they are going to leave behind in their resistance to the establishment of a new balance, while we all know that the precarious chaotic pseudo-order of the *Second Wave* or antithesis cannot be maintained, or we are all to perish.

Toffler sees this transition clearly as a revolutionary and perhaps bloody process, but anyway as a period of intense conflict. In *Powershift (1991)*, Toffler writes:

> A revolutionary new system for creating wealth cannot spread without triggering personal, political and international conflict. Change the way wealth is made and you immediately collide with all the entrenched interests whose power arose from the prior wealth-system. Bitter conflicts erupt as each side fights for control of the future. (Id., 10)

> Those who fought for control of the future made use of violence, wealth, and knowledge. Today a similar, though far more accelerated, upheaval has started. The changes we have recently seen in business, the economy,

politics, and at the global level are only the first skirmishes of far bigger power struggles to come. For we stand at the edge of the deepest powershift in human history. (Id., 11)

Chapter Two

The Restriction of National Sovereignty

Introduction

In the present chapter we are going to look at some examples and case law that demonstrate the fact that national sovereignty today is no more sacrosanct, as this was still the case before the 19th century.

Let me add here in a side note that *foreign sovereign immunity* should not be confounded with so-called 'state immunity,' while in the literature the two terms are often used synonymously. But they are not synonymous.

THE RESTRICTION OF NATIONAL SOVEREIGNTY

Sovereign immunity or state immunity regards the immunity of the national government vis-à-vis its own citizens, regularly in torts actions, when citizens have been harmed by civil servants, or by tax regulations or any coercive action done to the citizen by the state or federal authorities.

In such cases, the citizen can rightfully claim damages by suing their government in a torts action in front of an administrative court. Only in these cases, we speak of sovereign or state immunity.

The cases that I am going to reference hereafter in this chapter, however, involve *foreign* sovereign immunity, the immunity from jurisdiction a *foreign state* may enjoy in front of a tribunal in claimant's the forum state.

While both state immunity and foreign sovereign immunity are initially based upon the concept of *full national sovereignty*, they both have been severely restricted, if not eroded, which is a significant fact to note for the international law scholar in that such a situation *signals a paradigm change of even wider dimensions in the future.*

Why is that so? Let me explain. International law is widely built and developed by international practice, which is the way nation states behave on the international platform, both in bilateral and multilateral relationships.

What scholars and international law practitioners do, and also what judges do when they rule over questions that involve international law, is *not* lawmaking, it is a *not a normative behavior.* This is a very important fact to realize for the lay person, because otherwise the function of international law cannot be understood.

The only 'persons' that are allowed to actually be *normative* in international law are the states themselves, the former sovereigns, the modern nation states, and their state departments. Their behavior then, is carefully observed and registered by international lawyers, scholars and other state departments, for how they move around in the world, what they do, what they don't do, what they want to do in the future, all this has *normative quality*.

This is what actually forms and develops international law, it's called 'state practice,' in a short term.

One may find that quite outlandish as an idea, but when you think about it, it's only logical. Where there is no international government, and accordingly, no international parliament, the norms and rules are set by the nations, simply because they have 'no superior.'

That's why it's all so strange, it's also why it's all so interesting, so fascinating to study for a lawyer. It was for me, while I was never a passionate lawyer for domestic law, but European Law and International Law were for me as passionate topics to study as reading history novels or watch a documentary about the opium war.

Now, there is another subtle thing to note, that is the jurisprudence. We have an International Court of Justice in the Hague, Netherlands, but lay people often ignore that this court can rule only over conflicts resulting from international conventions *where the states member of that convention have expressly agreed to submit to the court any conflict arising from the treaty.*

THE RESTRICTION OF NATIONAL SOVEREIGNTY

That is why the courts that rule over questions of foreign sovereign immunity are national courts, in the United States, the District Courts.

Now, the interesting thing is that those courts must be very qualified as their judges must do actually the same work as international law scholars, that is, law professors accredited at reputed universities, and for the US District Courts, I must say, they do this work admirably well!

To repeat it, their judgments are *not normative* in the sense that their decisions would automatically form international law, while they are of course normative for the case pending at court; however, it is also true that when there is a *consistency of such jurisprudence over a considerable time*, and when such consistency covers not just one nation but the jurisprudence of a *number of nations*, agreeing thus on seeing certain things in a certain way, then we speak of a 'new rule in international law' that is built by state practice.

The courts did not by themselves make the rule, but in that their decisions were so constant over time, one must conclude that a *consistent state practice can be made out that over a certain time formed that new rule in international law.*

State Trading

An area where a clear restriction of national sovereignty was occurring is *international trade*, particularly with regard to commercial contracts where one party of the agreement is a private trader, and the other party, a foreign state.

THE RESTRICTION OF NATIONAL SOVEREIGNTY

While still two hundred years ago, governments hardly entered the marketplace for purchasing goods, and manufactured themselves all the goods and materials needed for their governmental purposes, this changed with the emergence of world trade during the 19th century. As a result, international law has widely changed from about the beginning of the 19th century.

Against the opinion of many skeptical international law experts, international law has stood trial as to its ability to flexibly adapt to paradigm changes in socioeconomic conditions as well as to the psychology of nations' behavior on the international stage.

Are we dealing with a law of sovereigns, or with a law of nations? How did sovereigns behave in the past, and how do our modern nation states behave?

THE RESTRICTION OF NATIONAL SOVEREIGNTY

When we look at these questions, we can observe a tremendous *shift in international jurisdiction* from about the last decade of the nineteenth century. This paradigm shift was subtly prepared by incidental precedents such as *The Schooner Exchange (1812) v. M'Faddon (1812), 11 U.S. [7 Cranch] 116, 135 (1812)* and culminated in a thorough reform of international procedural law.

Let me explain. Before the 19th century, sovereigns, or rulers, were considered immune from any jurisdiction other than their own. This was historically and politically a sound concept until the moment when, from about the middle of the 19th century, the young nation states engaged in the growing international market and behaved, as such, like traders.

In a specialized study, I elucidated the procedural questions, the evidence problems and the burden of proof in such litigations against foreign states and their agencies and instrumentalities.

> —Peter Fritz Walter, Evidence and Burden of Proof in Foreign Sovereign Immunity Litigation: A Procedural Guide for International Lawyers and Government Counsel (3rd Revised Edition, 2017).

The fact that the nation states entered the international marketplace for buying and selling goods set a novelty event on the timeline of human history.

International law was not prepared to deal with that novelty at first, and could not protect private traders from losing huge sums of money because they had contracted with a foreign government; what namely happened quite regularly in these cases was that the foreign government would invoke 'foreign sovereign immunity' in order to escape its liability under the contract.

The consequence of the immunity claim was namely that the forum state had to deny jurisdiction over the foreign state, and dismiss the claim because of a 'procedural handicap.' When a claim is dismissed on procedural grounds, the court *will not enter the substance matter* of the case, and thus not rule over the transaction that was at the basis of the claim. The lawyer would in such a case reason their client that 'the case cannot be won because of lacking jurisdiction.'

Thus what the new situation created was *rampant injustice,* and heavy financial losses of large trading companies around the world as a result of having contracted not with a private trading company but with a foreign state, or an agency or instrumentality of a foreign state.

One can figure that in the beginning courts were reluctant to affirm jurisdiction over foreign states, while they were well aware of the blatant cynicism of the situation. The novelty was overwhelming and they found international law had no instrument to deal with the problem. And as the topic was a sensitive one because the principle of national sovereignty was in play, judges tended to be very careful. They did not want to step on the feet of some or the other foreign government, and still less did they want to offend their state department or department of foreign affairs.

Some however were conscious that a historical break was about to happen and that it was more or less blunt injustice done to the private claimants *to grant immunity to a state who voluntarily engaged in the market place* and then pleaded sovereign immunity as a defense in an action that did not concern sovereign but commercial activities of that state.

As the business volume of most of those cases was considerable, judges soon found a way to avoid such injustice. They argued that it was *not the nature of the person* involved, speak the sovereign nature of the foreign state, that was decisive for the granting or not of immunity, but the *nature of the activity in question.*

That was after all a clever strategic move to go around the intricate sovereignty question. 'We are not going to touch the sovereignty of the state. We look what states are doing, and upon their acting they are judged, not upon their nature; their sovereignty thus remains untouched.'

The reasoning was brilliant and efforts of highly qualified international defense lawyers who worked pro immunitatem eventually failed. At that point, the law was changing, and nobody could prevent that tremendous paradigm shift from happening. International law was going to get a new face! It was almost a revolution, despite the fact that people other than government consultants and international lawyers had (and have) barely an idea of these affairs, as they are not catchy topics for the international mass media.

The lawyers who worked on the side of the private merchants argued that if the activity in question was by its nature commercial, the state was to be denied immunity and the foreign court had to affirm jurisdiction. If, however, the act or activity was sovereign, then immunity had to be granted and jurisdiction was to be denied.

That was indeed a handy rule that was quickly to become a sort of standard for judging sovereign immunity questions before national tribunals.

And the change of international law in this respect demonstrates that international law is well flexible and open to change, when change is needed to uphold justice and avoid flagrant injustice!

International conferencing, while it's today a popular topic in the international media, is not the primary lever for change in matters of international law. International law changes rather incrementally, and this most of the time *through case law*. This is exactly what happened with the development of the *restrictive immunity concept*.

The Restrictive Immunity Concept and the Burden of Proof

This concept evolved from the end of the 19th century until today, and this process is still ongoing, and all the details and modifications of this concept were worked out by case law in agreement with international law experts and scholars, international lawyers and consultants, not, or only to a minor extent, by international agreements.

One may imagine, even as a lay person, how important it is to know the allocation of the burden of proof in matters of sovereign immunity litigation, for it often is crucial for winning the case.

If, for example, the plaintiff bears the full procedural and substantial burden of proving the essentials of his claim, as it is under general civil law, and common law, then the restrictive immunity theory would not have gained much value in practice, as in most cases foreign states could go away with dishonoring commercial agreements, thus causing immense financial losses to the private sector.

Accordingly, among the array of questions I was essentially discussing in my study, the problem who bears the *burden of proof* in litigations where foreign sovereign immunity is claimed, was by far the most important.

The question of the burden of proof is originally not a matter of international law, but of the applicable national substantive law.

> —Cross on Evidence (1979), p. 87. See also Peter Fritz Walter, The Law of Evidence in a Nutshell: Basics for Law School (Scholarly Articles, Vol. 1, 2015/2017).

THE RESTRICTION OF NATIONAL SOVEREIGNTY

Needless to add that a case must have the necessary minimal contacts so that a national tribunal can affirm jurisdiction.

While under the United States' *Foreign Sovereign Immunities Act of 1976*, this question is stuck together with the question of the burden of proof, as a matter of legislative wording, minimal contacts is quite a different problem.

> — Public Law 94-583 (H.R. 11315), 90 STAT 2891-2898, 28 U.S.C. 1330, 1391, 1602-1611, 71 AJIL 595 (1977), 15 ILM 1388 (1976).

The interesting question comes up if, as a result of a quite homogenous national range of immunity laws, *international law was formed in a way so as to encompass today an evidence rule in the field of sovereign immunity?*

In my study, which is an editorial development and update of my 1987 doctoral thesis at the law faculty of the University of Geneva, I came to an affirmative conclusion, and time has given me right, as now the *International Law Commission* has codified the matter along the lines of my thesis conclusions, in the *United Nations Convention on Jurisdictional Immunities of States and their Property (2004).*

> *— Adopted by the General Assembly of the United Nations on 2 December 2004. Not yet in force. See General Assembly resolution 59/38, annex, Official Records of the General Assembly, Fifty-ninth Session, Supplement No. 49 (A/59/49).*

To begin with, let me present an example for the interplay between national substantive law and jurisdictional immunity, *as a matter of international law,* with respect to the burden of proof.

Lets suppose a private merchant claims damages for the repudiation of a contract signed with a foreign state. In such a case, there is today no question that the claimant bears the burden to proof as to the existence of the title, the contract. But who bears the burden of proof for the facts that determine the outcome of the question of foreign sovereign immunity?

Obviously, it would be easy if the burden here would also be on the claimant. It would simplify the evidence procedure. Unfortunately, things are not that simple. Even though often the two burdens may coincide, this is not always so, especially not under the *Foreign Sovereign Immunities Act of 1976 (FSIA)* of the United States.

Theoretically, there are two options to design the burden of proof for substantiating the sovereign immunity claim:

> i) the burden is on the plaintiff for demonstrating the commercial character of the transaction;

THE RESTRICTION OF NATIONAL SOVEREIGNTY

- ii) the burden is on the foreign state to prove that the nature of the transaction was exceptionally governmental.

I shall in the following summarize the main results of my analysis, without being too explicit; in fact in my doctoral thesis and my recent study I have effected a detailed comparative law analysis of all six immunity statutes that at the time were prevalent for assessing the content of international law on the matter.

Here only the general principle is of importance; when we see how, and how thoroughly, national sovereignty has been restricted, even if only in commercial matters, we see that the future is open for the creation of a world government.

The crucial condition for this to happen is lucid awareness of the *malignant cancer of national sovereignty*, a concept that hopefully will eventually be confined to safe boundaries.

THE RESTRICTION OF NATIONAL SOVEREIGNTY

A first and decisive step on this way were the following legal instruments, that were created between 1976 and 1982, and that are in my view important legal codifications regarding world democracy, in the true sense.

And interestingly so, once again the old insight was confirmed that commercial law and fair trade are the cornerstones for our world legal system to improve and evolve, because *trading is communication*, and as such it requires the *respect of human values* like free will, contractual freedom, *pacta sunt servanda* and legal predictability.

n the absence of these values, no world trade is possible; without world trade to function smoothly, the mere *idea of world government* would appear grotesque and nonsensical. The statutes subject to my comparative law study are:

- *The Foreign Sovereign Immunities Act, 1976* (United States)

- *The State Immunity Act, 1978* (United Kingdom)

- *The State Immunity Act, 1979* (Singapore)

- *The State Immunity Ordinance, 1981* (Pakistan)

- *The Foreign States Immunities Act 87, 1981* (South Africa)

- *The State Immunity Act, 1982* (Canada)

My scrutiny and comparison of these different national statutes on foreign sovereign immunity revealed *common principles on the allocation of the burden of proof* with regard to both immunity from jurisdiction and immunity from execution.

Before going more in detail, let me shortly explain the difference between 'jurisdictional' and 'executional' immunities. It's in fact

THE RESTRICTION OF NATIONAL SOVEREIGNTY

something so basic and common-sense that a lay reader can easily understand it.

When you sue a foreign state in your national jurisdiction, and the state invokes the foreign sovereign immunity claim, we are dealing with 'jurisdictional' immunity; if however you are a judgment creditor of that state, having already received a judgment against the foreign state that entitles you to receiving payment or indemnities, and you seek satisfaction, then we are dealing with immunity from execution.

In addition, there is an important variation of the latter constellation; for example you have done repairs of a foreign state's embassy in your country, and they don't pay the bill after you finished the work. Even before having a judgment against them, you want to *secure your interests* by seizing, by act of law, one of the embassy's bank accounts for your satisfaction; in such a case we are equally dealing with 'executional' immunities.

IMMUNITY FROM JURISDICTION

With regard to immunity from jurisdiction, the burden of proof is in principle on the foreign state to show some factual basis of its immunity claim by establishing a *prima facie case* of immunity.

This means the state must provide some evidence, not a full proof, for the court to affirm immunity and deny jurisdiction.

When forwarding evidence for establishing this prima face case, the foreign state is not obliged to disprove all immunity exceptions, but only the one(s) the plaintiff relies on. If the plaintiff does not specify exception(s) he relies on, the foreign state can generally affirm, by *affidavit* or otherwise, that it falls under the range of the statute, and thus—

- that it is a foreign state within the definition of the statute, and

- that the act or activity in question was of a public, governmental nature.

—The affidavit is the usual means of proof in all foreign sovereign immunity actions. Not only can the foreign state prove its prima facie case with an affidavit, but also the plaintiff can put forward affidavits and documents in support of its motion, Mol, Inc. v. People's Republic of Bangladesh, 572, F.Supp. 79, 82 (D.Or. 1983).

Once the foreign state has made its case, the evidential burden shifts to the plaintiff to prove the applicability of the exception(s) he relies on.

If the plaintiff fails to establish an exception to immunity, immunity has to be granted since the prima facie evidence provided by the foreign state erects a 'presumption of immunity.' If, on the other hand, the foreign state fails to show some prima facie basis of immunity, the ultimate burden or persuasive burden would be with the foreign state and immunity would have to be denied. This is however only so if the plaintiff, in his pleadings, has given convincing proof for the court to qualify the activity in question as *commercial*. Since, in this case, no presumption has been erected, and international law does not contain any presumption in favor of immunity or in favor of jurisdiction, the court cannot, without endangering the sovereignty of the foreign state, deny immunity without further enquiry and only on the basis of the burden of proof.

In this case, the court must namely qualify the activity in question *on the basis of all the evidence* the parties have submitted. The court is notably not allowed to refuse immunity only because the foreign state has not entered an appearance or otherwise failed to defend itself. The fact that the restrictive immunity doctrine imposes a certain rule of the burden of proof does not mean that the court is liberated from its obligation to rule *sua sponte (ex officio)* on the question of immunity.

The statutes slightly differ in the provisions concerning *agencies or instrumentalities* or *separate entities* of the foreign state.

Whereas the American and Canadian statutes assimilate agencies and instrumentalities, for jurisdictional immunity purposes, the British and related statutes split separate entities from the foreign state and erect a presumption of non-immunity to their effect.

Under the American and Canadian immunity statutes, the burden of proof, *without presumption,* is the same for agencies or instrumentalities of the foreign state.

THE RESTRICTION OF NATIONAL SOVEREIGNTY

In practice the results of the two different approaches however hardly differ as to the burden of proof, for the foreign state must, in its prima facie evidence, join some proof that the agency or instrumentality in question belongs to the foreign state, rather than being an entity distinct from it.

It is logical that the privilege of sovereign immunity is not granted to legal entities distinct from foreign states. That is why, in practice, the American and Canadian statutes can also be said to contain *presumptions of non-immunity* with regard to such distinct legal entities, despite the fact that the text of these statutes, as to the burden of proof, is less clear than the other enactments on foreign sovereign immunity.

Immunity from Execution

With regard to immunity from execution, the old rule that is called *absolute rule of sovereign immunity* has not been altered. It stayed intact as a true general rule of sovereign immunity, despite the fact that the statutes concede some exceptions to this rule, notably the absence of immunity if the property in question was used, by the foreign state, for (exclusively) commercial purposes.

Since the rule of immunity from execution is not only a residual concept, as is the rule of immunity from jurisdiction, no prima facie evidence is necessary from the side of the foreign state to erect this immunity rule into a true presumption.

Only the British, Pakistani and Singapore acts require to this effect a special ambassadorial certificate. But this requirement is no onus for foreign states and has not to fulfill the standards of a prima facie case. It is more of a formality, easily to be rendered by the head of the foreign state's embassy—a *simple statement* to the effect that the assets in question did not serve commercial purposes, but were used for the daily running of the embassy. Its effect is the erection of a presumption of immunity for the property in question.

The burden of proof for overcoming this presumption is squarely put in the lap of the judgment creditor, as it is the case under the statutes which do not contain such a certificate provision.

The normal evidence procedure, as the persuasive burden clearly remains with the judgment creditor, is such that the latter begins to present proof by submitting prima facie evidence that the property in question was used, by the foreign state, for commercial purposes. If the judgment creditor succeeds in establishing this *prima facie case*, the foreign state, by simply contradicting this proof, can be granted sovereign immunity, since the general rule of immunity from execution is on its side.

Even if the foreign state is not able to contradict the prima facie evidence of the judgment creditor, the latter must prove, by a preponderance of the evidence, the applicability of an exception to immunity from execution.

This is notably the consequence of ordinary rules of statutory construction that put the burden of proof on the one who struggles against a general rule contained in a statute.

This burden is *not met by prima facie evidence*, but only by a plain proof overcoming the presumption established under the general rule.

Thus, the *immunity risk* in matters of immunity from execution is clearly on the judgment creditor. In other words, the judgment creditor bears the *legal or persuasive burden of proof*. In any case of doubt (non liquet), the court must grant immunity. In other words, in matters of immunity from execution, the rule is *in dubio contra immunitatem*.

For certain types of property (military property or property of a foreign central bank), the statutes tend to be even more severe. They only differ in either refusing any execution (thus granting absolute immunity in the true sense) or permitting a very limited range of executory measures.

The Signal Function of Restricted Sovereignty

We have seen in our detailed analysis of the *restrictive foreign sovereign immunity doctrine* that the transition from the paradigm of 'absolute' immunity to the new standard of

THE RESTRICTION OF NATIONAL SOVEREIGNTY

'restrictive' immunity took more than a hundred years. That seems to be a very long time but is compared to the whole of human history a tiny event on the timeline of human evolution. And while as such it may have interest only for specialized lawyers, the signal function of this restriction of national sovereignty cannot be underestimated.

Notably, in English, a *restriction* connotes something being 'restrained' in its scope, power or expression.

We have seen that the once unlimited national sovereignty of a nation state today is restrained for the domain of jurisdictional immunities, when the activity in question was of a private, commercial nature.

When such a trend is to be traced, and corroborated by case law, and when the general idea has been accepted that sovereignty is *not per se an 'absolute' power,* but can well be restrained, and must be restrained when it brings harm to people, companies and to national economies, then we have a situation where, as lawyers say, a 'precedent was set.'

When a precedent was set, there is a likelihood that a similar constellation or situation will be judged *along the same lines* because of the similarity of interests or because the values to be protected are of a similar nature.

On the same line of reasoning, the text of the *European Convention on State Immunity*, 1972, states in its Preamble, that it takes into account 'the fact that there is in international law a tendency to restrict the cases in which a State may claim immunity before foreign courts'.

The *United Nations Convention on Jurisdictional Immunities of States and their*

THE RESTRICTION OF NATIONAL SOVEREIGNTY

Property (2004), contains a similar clause. These clauses are of course very general and have a mere declaratory character, but they are nonetheless important because of their signal function.

We have to keep in mind that only a hundred years ago such a clause in an international treaty would have been unthinkable as such an international convention wouldn't have been agreed upon; the majority of states would have thought of such a clause as 'offending their sovereignty.'

The concept of sovereignty has to be seen historically; the coming up of nation states was a Renaissance endeavor, and would again have been unthinkable during the Middle-Ages because of the Church's absolute power. But when the Church's power was restrained, the nation states took over the sacrosanct nature of the Church's absolute domain, and by creating the idea of 'national sovereignty' expressed their claim of almost divine 'untouchability,' and a set of absolute powers connected with it.

This is actually a good example for showing how cyclic human history is, and how nonlinear. It is cyclic in the sense that the same problems are put on the same stage but in the *disguise of different actors,* until humanity has gained enough consciousness to tackle the problem itself, instead of addressing the actor that embodies it.

Not the Church was bad but the concept of total dominion over subjects treated as vassals; not the nation states are bad but again the concept of absolute, and sacrosanct, *sovereignty* because it does harm to people, and to the smoothness of international trade, and the communication between peoples. Thus, we can say that

THE RESTRICTION OF NATIONAL SOVEREIGNTY

humanity has recognized 'the problem' twice, first in identifying the human rights abuses committed by the Church, second by realizing that absolute sovereignty, to mention only the commercial sector, brings heavy losses to private traders and a possible scenario of 'total injustice' into international trade, which cannot reasonably be tolerated.

As the problem of national sovereignty is larger, and does harm also in other ways than commercially, especially when we think that it is the single most dangerous trigger for wars between nation states, resulting in *heavy loss of human life*, the signal function given from the commercial sector is not to be overlooked and needs to be carefully analyzed by international law scholars and world peace organizations!

For me, as an international lawyer, the slow but steady erosion of national sovereignty is a

THE RESTRICTION OF NATIONAL SOVEREIGNTY

fact that cannot be overlooked, and that I myself consider as a positive trend, a road that leads into the right direction.

Currently, we are in a transition period until about the year 2020 during which the concept of national sovereignty *is going to do even more harm*, but also where human consciousness will considerably rise to acknowledging the perilous nature of the very construct of sovereignty.

This, then, will open the door to a modification and further restriction of sovereignty in the sense of restraining it by multilateral agreement, and giving a large part of sovereign national power over to a supranational body called 'world government' or otherwise.

Behold, this is *not a utopian idea* but already now a process and dynamics that cannot be overlooked! The fact that in the international media little is to be heard about it, has to do with the fact that the matter is politically sensitive because national pride and a whole bunch of chauvinist values are connected and associated with it.

In sensible matters of this kind, international diplomacy has developed a careful approach of incremental and careful progress that doesn't offend the main sandbox players, as so doing would in the long run only result in regional and international setbacks.

Chapter Three

The Empowered Citizen

An Important Meeting

Back in 1998, I was invited to Brunei, the small kingdom in South-East Asia, for a presentation to the Ministry of Interior; they were interested in a leadership training for their civil servants.

To be true, I was not little surprised about the forward-thinking attitude of these generally rather conservative Muslim leaders.

The seminar, I was told, should take the form of a *train-the-trainers* program, so as to give a totally new shape to their formation of all civil servants in the country.

THE RESTRICTION OF NATIONAL SOVEREIGNTY

As I had done such a training formerly for the government of Indonesia, they were interested in recruiting me as a trainer.

When we first sat at the meeting table, a department head of the Ministry of Interior held a short speech for opening the discussion. After a short polite introduction and welcome, he said this:

—We see that in the past, the civil servant was the murky, obedient and often brutal executive who would carry things through to the end, even if he's wrong, thereby often hurting citizens and making for a bad image of the government. We know that *we do not want* this kind of civil servant for the future! We think that today the citizen is not any longer the vassal of their government, but the *customer* of the government. Accordingly, we need a civil servant who is responsive, alert, civilized, humble, courteous, respectful and smart, and who lets our government appear as positive and caring in the eyes of our people. Can you help us to get there?

I felt humbled. Never would I have expected such a progressive position from the government of a country that on the international scene comes over as a political tyranny, with a 98% Muslim population, a powerful and perhaps despotic ruler family, and an administration that is so opaque that most journalists say they ignore the details when they report any news in the country.

And I had to acknowledge that our image of foreign states is so often veiled by prejudice and by quick judgments, while a culture, a society, a nation is a very complex thing, actually a living thing, an *organism*— not a machine.

It is obvious for any political observer today that nation states that formerly were known only to diplomats and international scholars, today can make big headlines with their extraordinary ideas. Whatever the image is that the world puts upon them, the reality may be very different. In other words, we are so accustomed to the best ideas emerging from our famous European and American universities that we often overlook to see them appear in a different cultural, social and political setting.

This may be humbling us at first sight, but we really have to get used to it because it will be the political reality of tomorrow.

The World Model Revisited

The European model, as we are going to see in this article, has only a limited validity. It has the validity of a 'primal scene,' so to speak, for a world government of the future, the validity of a model that was for the time being a good and necessary solution.

Fact is that Europe, at that time, was seen as 'the world,' because of their colonial powers; this was also a fact of international law. But international law has changed since then, and the world today is not anymore represented by Europe and European 'world politics.' Today world politics is global politics, and while the power and economic structures of course are still dictated by a few superpowers, this picture is currently changing.

It was quite visible during the economic crisis in 2008/2009 that nations that still some decades ago were treated as 'poor developing countries' had almost no negative effects in that crisis that ravaged European and American banks, businesses and private consumers.

THE RESTRICTION OF NATIONAL SOVEREIGNTY

In India, there was only a slight turndown, and Cambodia, the country where I live and work since more than ten years and where I am writing this book, had as good as no contrary effects.

One of the reasons for this astonishing situation is that Cambodia at that time did not yet have a stock market; another reason is that Cambodia is not indebted; the country has received huge amounts of money for restructuring their economy after the Khmer Rouge disaster, but that money was given unconditionally, not in the form of loans.

While this information never appeared anywhere in the headlines, it is significant to see that the reverse effects of large global crises may hit those most who have accumulated a lot of bad karma in the past, because of their oppressive and colonialist politics, and we are going to see small countries emerging more and more who will come up with new and original solutions and will reap great benefits when they can manage their resources and give real service to their citizens, and other nations's citizens they want to attract for bestowing upon them those services.

    For example, Cambodia has become a fine banking economy, with modern banks set in place, with a strong Central Bank that is modeled after the German central bank, that tightly supervises and controls all Cambodian banks, so that a maximum amount of safety is guaranteed for foreign investments and deposits. This being said, the restriction of national sovereignty as a project that may take *several more decades* for being accomplished, cannot be seen in a vacuum; it has to be seen as embedded in those structural changes that transform national economies to be more and more entangled with each other, more and more networked, more and more electronic and fluid, more and more volatile, ad hoc, 'mobile' and more and more transparent and 'unpolitical.'

It is an old fact that a free economy fosters communication and intercourse between peoples of different cultures, and thereby turns against religious and political fundamentalism.

This fact is notorious for example in how Venice was ruled by the Doges during the Renaissance in Italy, how rich they became, how independent from the Vatican, and how much this has benefited Venice, and Venetian lifestyle and culture. It was, compared to the Church-ruled other regions in Italy, a free lifestyle, with refined pleasures and arts being on top of the agenda. This can actually be seen as an early form of a *secular government* as it later became the model for the modern state, such as France, during the Renaissance, which is perhaps the prototype model.

Legal efforts to reform the *laws of consent* have been considered in all major industrial nations even though not much change has been implemented yet.

You may ask what laws of consent have to do with world economy, international law and world peace? Well, quite a lot.

The child is considered as a major business participant since about the second half of the 17th century. Children were needed in the *Industrial Revolution* as certain tasks, such as for example weaving fine textures, could only be executed, at that time, with using the small hands of a child. Children, from that time, were cruelly exploited, so rampantly actually that it triggered a dramatic change in the child-rearing paradigm.

THE RESTRICTION OF NATIONAL SOVEREIGNTY

After some years of this ruthless economically profitable yet child-abusive business paradigm going into the land in all of the major European capitals, a resistance movement was making itself felt, first through pointed conferences, and later through national and international cooperation, and a paradigm was formed that was later called 'child protection' and that was at first inspired for protecting children from child labor and from sexual exploitation.

This form of protection took quite a long time to become effective because of the poverty of the masses and the financial power of the industrial power holders, but by and by the conditions of the child worker improved, until eventually child labor was declared illegal in all Western industrial nations.

From about the 19th century to today, the power of the child as a consumer has risen, in that the industry targets children as their main addressees for publicity; however, at the same time the *power of the child as a full human* has drastically declined because the child is not so far being granted free choice relations, with the result that they see their intimacy and erotic experiences curtailed down for complying with the needs of the industry to become *prime consumers*.

This is about where we are at this moment. But I predict a further change, adaptation or expansion of the global consumer paradigm in that the child, given their privileged position in the economy, will be granted *more autonomy* in the future, and that means also, the power to have free choice relations, and to have a complete sex life.

I admit that the resistance is strong to that idea, not because of any so-called *morality concept*, which at present really is a fiction, but because of the necessity for the present consumer paradigm to change in order to match up with the growing power needs of children and adolescents.

The resistance to considering the child a full human is not a morality demand.

Genuine morality, which is founded upon respect of the difference of another fosters paradigms that are socially and sexually permissive. In native cultures around the world, it can be seen that genuine morality and spirituality does foster the emotional and sexual freedom of children, and their early autonomy and self-reliance. It can be seen in these native cultures that parent-child emotional entanglement as we experience it as the rule in our modern consumer economies is actually a perversion from the natural continuum.

Children today, in our modern economies, have the right and the power to have their MacBooks and iPods and they can browse more or less freely the Internet and can get their own information, instead of being restricted to the official media in form of national televisions, as this was still the case when I myself was a young boy.

This alone gives them a *tremendous power boost*, while this is hardly matched by the current educational paradigm that is still stuck in the past, with its insistence upon discipline, obedience and social compliance.

But most youngsters today go their own ways, and they develop their own creativity. This is an obvious fact of life today anywhere on the Internet.

I am now in my sixties and get comments to my Youtube channel from little boys or girls aged ten to fifteen, on a regular basis, be it

THE RESTRICTION OF NATIONAL SOVEREIGNTY

they are child prodigies, and are interested in my coaching services for pianists, or because they have their own unique political and social opinions and wish to voice them.

In general, my Youtube statistics showed me that my main audience is just 13 to 18, with only a few older people for some of my videos.

This fact honestly surprised me to a point it got me to deeply reflect on today's consumer economy and who actually drives it. I came to believe that children and adolescents in a way drive our economy and that is why, logically so, they are going to be empowered in the near and far future, and that the 'child protection' laws are going to be changed to their favor—and not, as many believe, for doing a favor to pedophiles, for we encounter here clearly two different policy agendas.

This being said, I believe that the *pedophile agenda* is a *fake agenda* as there is only *one* agenda that drives us forward as a society today, it's the child's agenda, not the childlover's agenda. It's the agenda of mother nature, that requires respecting the female and the child as part of the *female creator energy*, not the male dominator energy that was the reigning paradigm during the hubristic madness of patriarchy.

A Changing Social Framework

I am convinced that the future will bring real changes here because the present new generations need to grow up for implementing them. There will be more rights for elders, too, and a *more acute awareness* of the precious wisdom of elders through their communication and togetherness with children, as this was realized by Françoise Dolto in the 1980s in Paris, France.

THE RESTRICTION OF NATIONAL SOVEREIGNTY

—See Peter Fritz Walter, Françoise Dolto and Child Psychoanalysis (Great Minds Series, Vol. 4), 2015.

The young modern citizen simply feels more empowered to boycott social collaboration each and every time personal freedom is curtailed down by laws and regulations. This new citizen will more easily become a social reformer who doesn't shy away from contacting their president or senators for making social policy suggestions.

This also means that many of the existing forms of social police and denunciation that are undermining personal freedom and trust between people will be abandoned for allowing humanity to develop into a more trustful state of togetherness. It will be seen that peace can only be based upon *freedom, trust and abundant soul power of the individual,* and not upon ruthless competition, endless social and economical hierarchies, oligarchy, tyranny and persecution.

In fact, our mass media do all to prevent world citizens to gain this awareness as our present economies, and their marketing philosophies, are built upon the idea of the 'national state.' However, this monolithic structure is currently eroding more and more with the economic reality of a 'networked' world economy, where national segments are more and more intertwined with each other, and where the general entanglement becomes one of global dimensions.

It is obvious that the more our national economies are entangled with each other, the lesser are chances that because of national sovereignty conflicts, huge wars will be engaged, simply because the 'winners' and 'losers' can hardly be anticipated, and the danger of 'being hurt' when 'hurting others'

THE RESTRICTION OF NATIONAL SOVEREIGNTY

becomes a real global concern. It's as if we were all living together today in a huge elevator, and when we begin to shoot around, the danger is not just that we kill each other, but that the whole elevator will crash down.

When the transition from authority-based economies to *functional network economies* will be the order of the day, the concept of 'minority' will assume a quite different meaning as it had in the past.

It is no wonder that in a social system that sanctifies the power of the majority, the *in-group,* as the Bible reports it, there is huge individual and collective aggression toward the *out-group.*

This will be very different in the economies that are ahead of us and that are going to implement the leading economic paradigm of the future. In these economies, the division between *in* and *out* is no more valid as a *survival paradigm,* that it was indeed in ancient times, for the simple reason that today the survival paradigm of the future is the integrative solution that *embraces the difference* of the other, in that it embraces the whole of the market place.

When the market place is *global*, this means that there is no other solution than a *global humanity* on both the economical and the political levels. This new integrative and holistic paradigm, that of course got its major incentive from our integrative and holistic science, will automatically integrate cultural and ethnic dividers, and it will 'rationalize' all religious diversion to come to see the unity in diversity, and the diversity in unity.

This, then, will be the start of a global culture that is able to embrace and develop the idea of a *world government* as the ultimate solution for bringing us world peace.

An Uncanny International Organization

I am going to have a look at an *uncanny international organization* that was so far not being considered as such, yet which has the potential to help bringing about a democratic world government in the future. I am talking about the World Wide Web, the information highway, the Internet.

It seems to me that human intelligence which created the Internet is fundamentally different from all what we had before in human history.

The interesting fact about it is that not one man or woman has created it, but many, often simultaneously cooperating from different points of the globe.

The Web was thus perhaps the first really effective global institution we have created.

And that is why, among other reasons that I believe the Internet will grow beyond an information highway to become a *political highway* as well.

When we compare the Internet with another global institution, the United Nations, there are at least two striking differences.

The United Nations was a creation of states, at a government level, and not something growing from the base layer of societies.

The privileges or advantages that the UN provides were primarily intended for the *principi*, the former kings or rulers, and later for the nation states.

Let us not forget the fact that for the protection of the individual, international law still provides only a minimum standard. Human rights and the rights of minority

THE RESTRICTION OF NATIONAL SOVEREIGNTY

populations are protected *only within the range of special pacts or agreements*, such as the international conventions against torture, yet the nation states are free to join these international agreements or not.

The second, perhaps more important point of difference is that the United Nations, after their creation, have pretty much split into regional power groups.

It's not a coincidence that the European Community was another branch of the same tree, coming out of vision that people like Woodrow Wilson and, as we shall see further down, even philosophers like Rousseau and Kant had about the future of a united world.

At the same time, *European Integration* was pouring wine into the water of the original idea of a *Community of Nations* that is truly global.

That is why I believe the Internet is an *extraordinary creation,* for it has a far-reaching political potential. It is as if it had been created by an unconscious will, something like a *cosmic intention* that is beyond a merely human perspective.

When you observe the development of the Web and the fact that really Mr. Everyone and Ms. Shareware drive it forward to set new cultural and commercial standards, you can but be amazed about the power of the individual.

This may sound provocative. Yet we touch here a mystery that goes beyond all what we have observed hitherto on the globe, something that is like a new gospel, a new power, and a new global village for all.

So, to put it clearly, the Internet is the first international organization that really works in the sense of *res publica,* as the old Romans called political matters. And in that sense, as a forum for the public cause, the Internet really is *functional*.

Minorities, for example, be they racial, political or sexual, are effectively propagated through the Web. The police laws of most countries can prohibit minorities from gathering as long as the gatherings take place within local boundaries. But the police cannot legally control them when these gatherings are held online.

Since Web meetings are virtual, they do not fall within those laws. As a result it can be said that the Web created more democracy and freedom of speech.

However, this freedom also means that we have to use it responsibly. If we allow people to abuse of it, we jeopardize our newly gained privilege. International fundamentalism, secret services, right-wing movements, misguided groupings and a large mass of frustrated and negative individuals only wait for the chance to exert a tight control over the Web so as to install new and hitherto unknown forms of totalitarian government and rulership. The only effective way to prevent this from happening is that we exert responsible self-control in all forms of online publishing and virtual communication. This implies that we have to become conscious of the value that is linked to freedom and to simple and unprejudiced human communication.

    Instead, people seem to ask for more regulation and strict guidelines for conduct on the virtual space. This is however within the old paradigm. It means to restrict freedom once again because a certain amount of frivolous people are unwilling to use it responsibly. If we want to avoid this result, we have only one choice, either to provide

THE RESTRICTION OF NATIONAL SOVEREIGNTY

organizations with set regulations inviting people to become members for set purposes and to limit communication to set agendas and for set interests or topics, or to change the paradigm.

What is presently taking place on the Web is the first alternative. It means basically to create cages for people who have not learned to conduct themselves properly outside of those cages, and in full freedom.

Human history is a continuous up and down of times of more and less freedom. But at all times certain people have searched for cages because they were afraid of freedom or abused of it to the detriment of all.

However, it's not that difficult to live in wild life. While nature basically regulates itself automatically, by a process called *self-regulation*. I believe self-regulation, which has been found by systems research to be one of the most basic and most functional ingredients of living systems, will become a social and even a political value.

Now, let's shift our perspective from the economical to the political and have a closer look at that daring idea of the Web becoming, perhaps not too far in the future, a real *international organization and political forum* of all peoples in the world.

We know from the development of the European Union (EU) that the political union is very difficult to realize, and in fact the EU is far from being a political union with all what this would involve for its member states. The reason is probably that so much trustbuilding is required for a large number of people agreeing on implementing new systems of government or conceding national powers to a supranational organism.

THE RESTRICTION OF NATIONAL SOVEREIGNTY

The United Nations is a striking example for how *not* to do it correctly. They were from the beginning set to implement a political unification with, in the future, ideally, a world government. However, the anxieties were and are so high that the courageous goals were pursued less than half-heartedly. The end result was that bad compromises were made, compromises that really were compromising the whole idea and led to an absurd reality which counts as its major fact the largest bureaucracy in the world, engendering an irresponsible waste of resources.

But let me ask, where is the Web heading?

You may object that it is too far-fetched to admit that the Web could eventually bring about what both the European Union and the United Nations did not achieve: a world community, a union of nations, of peoples. How can?

If we take a closer look at this seemingly Utopian idea, we see that there is a fundamental difference between the European Union and the United Nations, on one hand, and the Web, on the other, in their respective ways to realize this global union of peoples.

The difference is the fact that the Web begins at the basis whereas all other present international organizations began at the top. What do I mean?

On the Web, masses of people from different cultures get into communicating with each other, first for research or academic purposes, then for business, the exchange of goods and services, and eventually for simply getting to know each other, looking at one another's home pages, learning from each other, communicating basic needs, feelings and opinions. The trend is that the Web becomes every day more a meeting place for a *large variety of people* communicating for a *large variety of purposes.*

While in the beginning the user had to write out every single command, with the graphic interface of the World Wide Web things became really simple and intuitive. In the meantime, also nonliterate people are able to write: they'll just talk and the computer will write for them.

I already pointed out that existing international organizations, despite the fact that they were instituted to unify peoples, have begun their work with the top classes of society, the rulers, kings and later the sovereign states, and not really seven billion individuals. If we build a house from the roof, forgetting about its foundation, its basis, the house will crash before it is ready. This is the true reason why neither the European Union nor the United Nations accomplish in reality what they have been created for: it's simply because they were established as *roof structures with a pitiful lack of foundation.* They came about through governmental collaboration and agreements, and not as a result of the will and the work of the peoples who have set these governments in place. They have not grown from the base layer of society, but from its top range.

That is why I am convinced that the Web will be the foundation for the *true union of peoples* in not too distant a future.

The Web grew without any governmental control, although it was, paradoxically, created for governmental purposes. Yet from the moment it was given to the public by the military agencies that had created it, it was a free landscape for new discoveries. And it

THE RESTRICTION OF NATIONAL SOVEREIGNTY

quickly grew beyond national borders and cultures.

My idea may seem uncanny. Consider that also on the national level, stability was reached only from the moment that the peoples themselves chose their governments.

This is not so much a function of the constitutional system which can be monarchical or republican. As long as a king or ruler is firmly based upon the trust of his people, his government will bring about effective solutions and bear fruits.

Some of the old Chinese kings who based their rulership upon the true interest of their people and universal laws have given abundant evidence to this historical and political fact. On the other hand, the best republican government that is corrupt and has lost the trust of a majority of citizens will disappear sooner or later and leave a vacuum of frustration and a bad taste in the mouth of the populace.

What only counts is that the system is truly democratic, which means not just democratic on paper. On both the national and the international level, democracy brings about stability. Governments who do not enjoy the backup of their peoples reign in *unstable conditions* and can be thrown over by social unrest and upheaval.

Present international organizations are for the great majority established 'from above,' without democratic elections from the side of the peoples, in a process that is not transparent to the citizen. This is one of the reasons why the 'man in the street,' be it in the West or the East, when asked about the United Nations or similar organizations, either admits ignorance and gives a negative or indifferent judgment. This is simply so, and

THE RESTRICTION OF NATIONAL SOVEREIGNTY

understandable because they have not been directly involved in the creation of the organization or the election of its staff. How can these organizations then seriously attempt to build a future world government?

They would reign over people who do not even know them. Therefore, if these organizations, as it seems now, are unable to allow reforms, they will disappear.

That is why a few years ago the *European Parliament* was fundamentally reformed and direct elections for the European parliamentarians have been institutionalized. In the public opinion all over Europe this step was considered as a progress of the unification progress, although skepticism prevailed as to how the European Union will practically carry out the will of the peoples at its basis, and not only the will of their governments or top-class industries.

The Web has grown from the root up, and not from the branches down, as all present political international organizations did. Therefore, the chance that my prediction will come true is, I think, higher than the chance that it will not.

For it is much easier and much more effective to learn a healthy body perform more functions than to teach a sick and dysfunctional body to perform even very few basic functions. And the present international organizations are not only sick and dysfunctional, they waste human and financial resources to an extent that their maintenance equals ruin for all those who, willingly or unwillingly, have to finance them. And that is all of us.

Chapter Four

The United States of Europe

Introduction

In this last chapter we are going to see that the idea of world government, of a unification of peoples, and for the purpose of bringing peace is not new. It was contained in the so-called *peace plans* drafted by European philosophers back in the 18th century; since then, the unification idea has fueled a constant progress toward peace and peaceful cooperation among European countries.

For all those who are still critical about Europe, the fact should be considered that since 1945, there was no more war between the nations that are members of the *European*

THE RESTRICTION OF NATIONAL SOVEREIGNTY

Union (EU) and the treaties that preceded the union, the *ECSC (1951)* and the *EEC (1957)*.

While the European integrative process was surely not smooth, and while there is still much to criticize, the unification of Europe was successful by and large, and it has given peace to peoples who formerly were constantly battling with each other for centuries.

We are going to have further proof in this chapter for the fact that the major problem in world politics is not the racial, ethnic or cultural difference of peoples, but the institution of *national sovereignty*, as a power structure that is very much prone to being abused.

Interestingly enough, this was seen by those European philosophers, Kant, Rousseau, and others already after about *the first two hundred years* of national sovereignty having become a doctrine in international law. It was from about the 16th century, with the decline of the Church's power during the Renaissance, and with the need to form strong secular governments that the doctrine was gradually set in place, in the main European nations, Germany, France and Italy.

Generally, the publication of Machiavelli's political novel *The Prince (1513)*, is seen by international law scholars as a mark stone for the establishment of the *doctrine of national sovereignty* in international law and practice.

Until the 18th century, it had become obvious to political observers and realistic philosophers that the doctrine of national sovereignty, and the mere fact that those modern governments were secular for the most part, did not bring the desired benefits.

One of the initial ideas behind the establishment of strong secular governments

THE RESTRICTION OF NATIONAL SOVEREIGNTY

was to avoid religious wars that had devastated Europe during the Middle-Ages, and under the politically flawed regime of the Church. The idea was indeed that national sovereignty would bring more peace, by avoiding religious conflicts, wars and civil wars.

But it was unfortunately a shortsighted view for each of those strong secular regimes, then, wanted to gain the overhand in Europe, with the result that warfare continued, and became even more devastating than ever before in Europe. And we all know that it continued all through the centuries until 1945!

Thus, we can say Europe is an interesting forum for testing ideas, and we can conclude, contrary to the many black seers today, that the idea of unification was bringing peace to Europe while preserving national identities, cultures, languages and customs.

In fact, this is the main argument among today's youth against the idea of world government; they fear that a unification of the globe would lead to an Orwellian global system that would suppress personal freedom and lead to a kind of global Nazi empire. The voices are strong, and one has to browse only Google, Youtube and other popular forums to see what young people today think of the idea.

It seems to me that *conspiracy theory* has become so popular that at the end of the day, it's difficult to make out what is reality and what is conspiracy. In fact, these masses of people have rarely looked over the fence of their own cultural, political and social conditioning, and they have rarely investigated the details of human political history. If they had, they would see that war, while it's triggered by political and economic greed, is regularly sold to the masses with psychological arguments that stress the *difference* of the other nation, and that paint that other reality in blacker notes than the one 'at home.'

This was very well visible in the history of World War II, where about every nation involved in the war game indulged in *demonizing the other nations,* those on 'the other side,' while painting rosy images for those nations one was allied with.

The masses rarely know what the real motivations are for triggering wars, and who actually gains all that money with war; what they get to see and to hear is the psychological rhetoric that targets at demonizing those one wishes to attack and subdue. This argument is valid both for what at that time was called by Hitler 'the outer enemy' and 'the inner enemy.' The rhetoric of the Nazis was namely to demonize the Jews as the main 'inner enemies,' which is the strategy that eventually resulted in the Holocaust.

Thus, it has to be seen that the main danger in all of this is that people do not really know who are those beyond the fence, what kind of people they are, what they think and do, what they believe to be true, and so forth.

They imagine them to be very different because of their lacking knowledge about them, and that is why they can easily be brought to believe that those others are 'evil' or 'more evil' than oneself.

It is no wonder then that people who enjoyed higher education, and who have traveled much, who speak different languages, are seldom manipulated into becoming haters and persecutors, or war mangers. It is always those who know little, who have seen and heard little, and who ignore the main truths about the commonality of all human beings, as a matter of cosmic resonance, as a matter of the basic harmony within all of creation.

The war mangers exploit that lack of knowledge of the masses, to get them where the political and economic leaders want to get them, and this manipulatory process is much more difficult to stage *once peoples are unified in one land* without national borders, without passport controls, and without national newspapers that use to emphasize the 'goodness' of one's nation and their people, and the 'strangeness' of the other nations and their people.

The argument that 'national identities' have to be preserved is a fallacy. It is exactly that hypothetical and illusory fiction of national identity that leads to all those wars.

There is no such identity, and if there is, *it has been put up as a matter of constant ruthless propaganda*, for the very purpose of leading the people to the next war.

People have customs, they have personal, ethnic, religious and regional identities, they may have clan identities as well, as one can see in Italy or Corsica, they certainly have cultural identities, but not by nature a national identity. Hence, the harmful element is the national identity because it is the psychological mirror of national sovereignty.

When national sovereignty is voluntarily restricted by the nation states member of a world government, national identities will be gone if not from one day to the other, but within a few months or years, they will be dissolved, while the other identities will be kept in place.

It may be useful during the first years of such a government to actively emphasize the cultural identities of the peoples, in the sense a Hopi native recently communicated it to me.

He said that the Hopi idea of peaceful togetherness was indeed one where there is 'diversity within unity,' and that their leaders, when they emphasize peace and unity, always also emphasize the cultural diversity of the different tribes.

The Plans for 'Eternal Peace'

It has been observed since the beginning of the Iraq invasion that the political weight of the European Union (EU) and the process of *European Integration* were never before of greater and more global importance than at that moment in human political history.

In fact, had the union reached not only a certain amount of economic integration but also *political integration* with a central European government and an established foreign politics, the outcome of USA's offensive war declaration against Iraq might have been different.

International law experts notably unite in the opinion that the United States has violated fundamental principles of international law by their invasion in Iraq, and this not only because it disregarded to comply with the advice and measures of the United Nations' Security Council, but for more general reasons.

And here we are only talking about the invasion as such and not about the nowadays much more discussed fact that the US occupation powers systematically violate human rights on an almost daily basis by harassing the Iraqi population and mistreating prisoners of war, denying fundamental civil rights and fair trial to them.

As the leading socioeconomic and political powers in present-day Europe, led by France and Germany, were and are against a unilateral world-policing superpower USA that forces each and every opponent or pseudo-opponent to knee-jerking 'world democracy,' a third political power block next to America and Asia, however it may be called, represents a potentially paradigm-shifting lever for bringing about a large-scale landslide on the political and strategic world map.

It is a well-known fact that France under a courageous and self-assured President Jacques Chirac played a particularly preponderant role in contradicting George W. Bush's foreign policy concept for the Middle East, unveiling it as a badly masked invasion strategy with a neocolonial base intention.

It makes a fundamental difference when on the international scene not a single nation state dares to oppose the United States' hegemonic world power, but a whole political, economic and military block of two dozens of nation states. This block that a politically unified Europe could represent in the future, is of amazingly similar dimensions as the United States, both in terms of size and economic prowess.

And the people who drafted these peace projects were no lesser than the greatest philosophers of Europe, or perhaps of humanity, and they certainly are considered as highly integer by United States citizens as well.

THE RESTRICTION OF NATIONAL SOVEREIGNTY

In this sub-chapter, I shall have a look at what historically were the common roots of both the process of *supranational* and of *international* integration. Many today seem to have forgotten that the original impetus for founding a united Europe was first of all to establish an international political system suited for purporting peace, stability and growth for *all nation states,* regardless of their military might and their economic and political power.

The early peace projects were unanimously targeting at bringing about a new era of peace, nothing less and nothing of lesser value for all of us, that is, for the world community, not just for Europe. It is important to note this as the starting point, because it shows the human, and truly international intention of the early fathers of the world peace idea.

THE UNITED STATES OF EUROPE

I will first present the peace projects drafted by Abbé de Saint-Pierre, Jean-Jacques Rousseau, Immanuel Kant, Saint-Simon and Coudenhove-Kalergi that were intended at bringing about a European confederation—of whatever structure and political form—with the single most important focus to facilitate the peace process between nation states that historically have always fought against one another.

That is why these plans or projects for a *European Constitution* are simply called 'peace plans' in the international law literature. And when we consider the quite notorious international debate on the occasion of the invasion of the United States in Iraq, we cannot close our eyes in front of the political reality that a historical chance for establishing a peaceful world community has been missed at the onset of the 21st century. It was hopefully not missed forever.

Abbé de Saint-Pierre

The peace plan of the French Abbé de Saint-Pierre, presented in his *Mémoire pour Rendre la Paix Perpétuelle en Europe (1713)*, literally translated as *Memo for Establishing Eternal Peace in Europe*, foresaw a 'Confederation of all European Sovereigns.' The unified Europe was projected to be directed by a federal government.

> —See the summery in: Claude-Henri de Saint-Simon & Auguste Thierry, De la réorganisation de la société européenne (1814), Livre Premier, Chap. II, III in the edition of the Centre de Recherches Européennes, Lausanne 1967, pages 36, 37.

This plan stipulated in its five main articles that—

- Representatives of the contracting member states are going to be members of a permanent congress;

- The number of the voting sovereigns and those that are invited to join the convention is to be established;

- Each member state is to receive a guarantee safeguarding his territorial property; by the same token, the sovereign, his family and his premises are to be protected both against foreign invaders and rebellion from the side of his own vassals;

- The congress is functioning as the highest judge regarding the rights of the member states;

- The community is to be enabled to proceed with armed forces against each and every member state that breaks the convention, as well as against public enemies. (Id., 37, Translation mine)

This early plan already contained the idea of creating a *supranational authority* to be assigned precisely outlined powers and competences, while it must be conceded that these competences were in last resort depending on the goodwill of the sovereigns member of the convention. Obviously, the guarantee of each sovereign's personal and territorial power seemed to have been the main focus of the draft convention. Interestingly, we know through historical research that this point (point three of the draft convention) was added later to the draft by Abbé de Saint-Pierre, namely in the hope of giving a stimulus to sovereigns to join the convention.

Jean-Jacques Rousseau

The project of a European government was a preoccupation of no lesser a mind than Jean-Jacques Rousseau.

He discussed the plan of Abbé de Saint-Pierre in his draft convention entitled *Extrait du Projet de Paix Perpétuelle de Monsieur l'Abbé de Saint-Pierre (1761)*.

—Jean-Jacques Rousseau, Oeuvres complètes, Vol. 2, Paris: Seuil, 1971, 333-352. Literally translated

'Excerpt of the Eternal Peace Project of Mr. Abbé de Saint-Pierre.'

Starting from a rather pessimistic outlook on the will of European sovereigns to ratify such a wide-ranging supranational agreement, thereby renouncing some of their sovereignty, he wrote in 1758 in the *Fragment sur le Projet de Paix Perpétuelle*:

> One must be as simple-minded as Abbé de Saint-Pierre for proposing the slightest innovation in whatever government in the world …
>
> —Id., p. 347. In his novel Émile, Rousseau bites even more heavily referring to the famous priest as somebody with 'great projects and little insights.'

Rousseau argued that common sense or 'reason' was not enough to ban future wars and instead required a clear and unequivocal subordination of the partner states under the newly created supranational federal government in exactly the same way as

THE RESTRICTION OF NATIONAL SOVEREIGNTY

individuals are subordinated to their home country's government. And that Rousseau's ideas were not bleak and blank propositions, but had realistic impact is to be seen in the precise wording of the conditions that Rousseau puts on paper:

- A federal government with singular and precise competencies;
- A federal legislation that is directly binding;
- A federal executive power with coercive competence over member states;
- A cohesion of the confederation so high that in the long run federal interests are going to prevail over national interests. (Id., 340)

Rousseau summarizes the advantages of the project in eight points, among which the points five till eight merit particular attention:

- Freedom of trade as well as safety in the trade between member states;

- Reduction of the defense budget and economic gain in times of peace;

- Advancement of agriculture and prosperity for the member states' rulers. (Id., 347)

Rousseau proved to be particularly lucid with regard to the details of Abbé de Saint-Pierre's peace convention, but argued that 'the thousand little difficulties will eventually all be levied when an enterprise of this grandeur is going to be put in practice.' (Id., 341)

He also recognized the crucial point that supranational agreements have integrative power not because of any coercive force involved in their establishment, but from the fact that the nation states deliberately *restrain their sovereignty* to convey that supranational or international organism a sovereignty of its own.

THE RESTRICTION OF NATIONAL SOVEREIGNTY

Rousseau was realistic enough to consider that modern nation states, despite the obvious advantages of supranational agreements, are very reluctant in practice to make concessions with regard to their sovereignty.

In his posthumous published writing *Jugement sur le Projet de Paix Perpétuelle (1782)*, Rousseau reflects about the possible interests that nation states might bring in play. And he distinguished between a real and an apparent interest *(intérêt réel et intérêt apparent)* in those states' political action.

Rousseau saw the 'real interest' realized when a peace convention was eventually ratified; the 'apparent interest' was the secret wish of every single sovereign involved in the negotiations to gain privileges and advantages that the others are deprived of.

The reason for this ambiguity was, according to Rousseau, the feudal system which made him conclude that a supranational federal government was, if ever, to be brought about through a *revolution*. (Id., 348 ff.)

This means that, ultimately, Rousseau doubted that the nation states would deliberately, and voluntarily, renounce a large part of their sovereignty for the creation of a world government; he rather speculated that the latter would, if ever, be brought about through chaos, upheaval, and violent transformation of the political status quo.

Immanuel Kant

The German philosopher Immanuel Kant published his peace project *Zum Ewigen Frieden* in 1795, during the last days of the French Revolution.

THE RESTRICTION OF NATIONAL SOVEREIGNTY

—Kants Werke, Band VIII, Abhandlungen nach 1781 (1923), 341-386. Literally 'For Eternal Peace.'

This is a suspicious coincidence when you remember what Jean-Jacques Rousseau had predicted as a condition for world peace. The first two articles of this draft read:

- The constitution in all member states shall be republican. (Id., 349)

- International law is to be based upon a confederation of free states. (Id., 354)

It is interesting to read about a European confederation being established for the first time not in 1951, but in 1795 and thus one hundred fifty years before the first step of *European Integration* that still today is not entirely realized, as we have *not yet reached political unification.*

We should have a closer look at these two main articles of Kant's convention. What is highly interesting, even from today's perspective, is the fact that Kant recognized what might be called the *internal setup of the member states* (Article 1) to be equally important as their togetherness on the international stage (Article 2). The internal setup, the 'constitutional software' as it were of a nation state is what Kant considered to be the hanger of the whole convention.

We have had enough experience to know today that indeed without a democratic base setup within each member state, their peaceful togetherness is highly unlikely. We have good historical examples for the lucidity of this view when we look at Europe, on one hand, and the United States, on the other.

The United States realized the *Republican Constitution* within the first state member of the new confederation, after the break with England. This first state of the confederation, *nomen est omen*, was *New England*.

THE RESTRICTION OF NATIONAL SOVEREIGNTY

The creation of the United States of America, with all the prosperity and power this creation was going to bring to its citizens and the world, was possible because all member states were modeled after the prototype of New England, and thus got *state constitutions* with clearly defined civil rights and constitutional guarantees for the citizen.

What happened in Europe? War.

Kant and Rousseau were right in that the feudal system was incompatible with the European unification process; what happened was that the social injustice inherent in feudalism rendered every attempt for peace an illusion for a long time to come.

When we see what cruel and destructive wars were to occur after Kant's and Rousseau's death in Europe until 1945, we get an idea of how painful, slow, incremental and important the unification process was for Europe, until today.

Behold, Kant and Rousseau did not have utopian ideas! Ideas are seeds that fall on soil that is either fertile or not. And often in history ideas fall in soil that is not fertile at the time the ideas come up. As with time and effort, the field was again and again plowed, the soil became more and more fertile, until one day the seed was able to grow. It's like that with all ideas, so why should it have been different with the great idea of a unified Europe?

Today, matters look not bad after all. We have achieved to bring about a *European Union (EU)* with more than forty members and considerable economic power. This union was peaceful since 1945 and thus, what was a rare exception in pre-20th century Europe, there were no more internal wars since seventy years. Furthermore, efforts are presently made

THE RESTRICTION OF NATIONAL SOVEREIGNTY

to draft a directly binding *European Constitution*, which admittedly failed in the first run but that will eventually succeed with the growing insight in the enormous responsibility that we all bear for bringing about this important step toward peace in European history, and by extension and analogy, in world history.

To summarize, when we compare Kant's project with the draft conventions of Abbé de Saint-Pierre and Rousseau, we can say that the French and Swiss philosophers had a keener and more realistic outlook on the future of Europe, and that their proposals were also of higher practical value, more detailed and more down-to-earth than the somewhat idealistic and high-strung plan by Immanuel Kant.

THE UNITED STATES OF EUROPE

Saint-Simon

Contrary to the previously discussed projects that intended to bring about a unified and pacified Europe through a union of their sovereigns, and thus by forming something like a *supranational government*, the proposal submitted by Saint-Simon was targeting much more at a unification of the *peoples* that were going to form the basis for that European Union. In fact, we can make out two possible ways to bring about a European confederation:

- Unification from above, through imposing a supranational government;
- Unification from below, through a peaceful democratic union of the peoples.

The plan of Count Saint-Simon, published in 1814, was to create Europe *from the bottom up*, not from the top down.

>—Claude-Henri de Saint-Simon, De la réorganisation de la société européenne (1967),

> Livre Premier, Chap. II, III. The rather long title of the proposal was 'De la Réorganisation de la Société Européenne ou de la Nécessité et des Moyens de Rassembler les Peuples de l'Europe en un seul Corps Politique en Conservant a Chacun son Indépendance Nationale, de Claude Henri de Saint-Simon et son élève Auguste-Thierry (1814).'

The title of the draft suggests a unification and confederation of the *peoples* that form the European soil; the solution was a political union that started at the very root level of society. Such a constitution 'from below,' the plan projected, was to start the unification process by creating a European parliament *(parlement européen)*. The idea was that as a matter of analogy, a union of peoples was to be created in much the same way as the union of *one people*. When one nation needed a national parliament with representatives for all its citizens, a unified body of peoples needed a supranational parliament with representatives of all the peoples of the union that was forming the legislative body for the confederation.

This requirement that today is fully realized, was indeed inspired by a keen sense of political realities. Saint-Simon concluded that without such a parliament, all, in the future of Europe, was again but a result of the power play of the European rulers.

The plan also contained one of the base principles of an *integrational model,* which is the creation of independent European institutions with precisely described competences.

Saint-Simon, just like Rousseau and Kant, started from the premise that as a first step a republican regime was to be founded in each of the future member states of the confederation. The formulation of this goal in the plan can be taken as the classical functional description of a parliament:

THE RESTRICTION OF NATIONAL SOVEREIGNTY

Count Saint-Simon
> There must be a coactive force that unifies the singular intentions, orchestrates the movements, transforms interests as propitious for the common good and solidifies commitments. (Id., 38)

Saint-Simon's idea that a European confederation could be created only from the moment that a republican regime was established in each member state is interesting because it predicted the future in some way.

We have seen the problem broadly discussed with regard to Turkey's anticipated membership of the European Union. While Turkey has a republican constitution, the human rights abuses that Turkey is internationally blamed for might be an obstacle on both a political and integrational level. The public discussion has made it clear that no member state of the EU is willing to tolerate a state-member that openly or in hidden ways sabotages civil rights or fosters totalitarian ways of government.

The difference to the setup of the United Nations is striking here as under the United Nations Charter, the form and nature of the internal government of each member state would belong to the 'internal affairs of that state' and thus not justify any action from the part of the other members states, Art. 2 (4) United Nations Charter.

This is a good example to show how different the United Nations are from the European Union in that European Integration was from the start understood as a process that requires *a much higher level of coherence and homogeneity* from its member states than the United Nations.

Another point of interest in discussing Saint-Simon's plan is the biting criticism of the peace project by Abbé de Saint-Pierre.

THE RESTRICTION OF NATIONAL SOVEREIGNTY

Joining Rousseau in the reproach that the priest's proposal was to rigidify and perpetuate the feudal system, there are four points that Saint-Simon derives from the Church's organization:

- A unified conception of *national and supranational* governmental structures and competences;

- A total independence of the supranational government from the national governments;

- Motivation of the supranational government should be rooted exclusively in common interests, and not in partial interests of certain member states;

- Public opinion within the community as the only guide post for the action of supranational government and parliament representatives. (Id., 39)

These maxims are of an astounding lucidity and have not lost a bit of their originality to this very day. In fact they are fully valid and applicable still in our present societies, and we can observe that they are often not respected in the daily running of the European Union.

Only in one point Saint-Simon's view was a bit too limitative. He saw the function of the European Parliament exclusively in resolving conflicts between member states, overlooking that the main function of a parliament is its legislative power, and that conflict resolution traditionally is better placed in the hands of diplomacy and direct personal contacts between head of states. But apart from this single limitation, Saint-Simon's plan is of high value and has certainly given flesh to the present integration model.

In addition, and contrary to Abbé de Saint-Pierre, Rousseau and Kant, Saint-Simon saw the functional and dynamic character of European Integration, its constancy and incremental character characterized by

THE RESTRICTION OF NATIONAL SOVEREIGNTY

moving from one stage of integration to the next.

He saw the beginning of the confederation in a union of the British and French parliaments to *one common parliament,* in which at a later stage the German parliament should join.

This was historically the first time that the idea of a *gradual process* of European integration was invented and elaborated, and we can clearly see today that this idea was the one that was going to be realized in Europe from 1951 until today, and not Rousseau's extravagant idea of bringing about peace and stability through a bloody revolution.

The aftermath of the French Revolution, as we all know, has shown that in fact the feudal structures were only labeled differently but that in substance nothing changed—only that many people lost their lives for an idiotic political reform that decapitated undesired heads only to put even more undesired heads in their place.

But the French revolution and also the German revolution of 1848 taught European self-thinkers and honest politicians that a unification of Europe was not going to be brought about through revolutions, bloody or unbloody, but through gradual change, flexible renewal, constant good-will and a step-by-step process of social, economic and political *integration*.

Today, every single head of state in Europe is convinced of this reality, and this insight makes the strength of Europe, and to a much lesser extent our economic or future political power. We have grown from our sandbox games into more mature relationships, and such a process can only create results through deep reflection and a strong effort to putting the past behind, not through quick-tempered decisions and emotional turmoil.

And this poised condition and self-assured outlook into the future is mirrored in the Charter of the EEC, Art. 237, 1 where we read that *'every European state can apply for membership in the community.'*

COUDENHOVE-KALERGI

After the catastrophe of World War I, and in a situation where a keen sense of realities replaced 19th century idealism, a new voice was to be heard that was fueled by a true passion for Europe and for democracy, the voice from inside the deepest of all resistance movements against Hitler and fascism was the voice of *Count Richard N. Coudenhove-Kalergi* in his book *Paneuropa* (1926).

THE UNITED STATES OF EUROPE

The most interesting aspect of the book is the clear insight that a united Europe will, if ever, be brought about only through a gradual process of *integration*.

> —Richard N. Coudenhove-Kalergi, Paneuropa (1926), Chapter XI, 1, p. 140. 'Pan' connotes 'all,' 'entire' or 'whole.'

The author sees this gradual process realized through four consecutive steps:

- The creation of a pan-European conference;

- The conclusion of an obligatory arbitrage and guarantee agreement;

- A European customs unification for bringing about a European economic union;

- The realization of the *United States of Europe* after the example of the *United States of America* through a pan-European Constitution and a supranational parliament consisting of two houses: the Congress and the House of Representatives. (Id., 140-142 (Translation mine)

THE RESTRICTION OF NATIONAL SOVEREIGNTY

In no previous plan for a European integration the various phases of a step-by-step building of the community were pointed out with that precision and clarity. In so far, the integrational draft convention by Coudenhove-Kalergi can be seen as the antithesis to Rousseau's constitutional model.

In the years to come, the pan-European ideas were motivating and fueling the resistance movements not only against Hitler, but also against Mussolini in Italy and the Vichy regime in France. These peace plans, that were further elaborated in the anti-fascist underground between the two world wars were directly flowing into the European integration dynamism of post-World War II.

> —See, for example, Pipkorn in Beutler/Bieber/Pipkorn/Streil, Die Europäische Gemeinschaft (1982), 1.2.2, p. 30. See more generally, Walter Lipgens, Europa-Föderationspläne der Widerstandsbewegungen 1940-1945 (1968).

Integration vs. Constitution

With the *European Community for Coal and Steal (Montan Union)* in 1951, the historical foundation was laid for the prototypical realization of a *European unification* in a relatively restricted, but economically important sector.

> —After the draft elaborated by Jean Monnet and Robert Schuman, the Montan contract was signed in a summit of the six founding members of the European Community on April 18, 1951 in Paris.

The subsequent creation of the *European Economic Community (EEC)* in 1957 was a significant step ahead toward integration through the integrative vision of both the European Court of Justice and the European Parliament.

> — See Art. 2 and Art. 3 EEC Charter where some 'tasks of the community' are enumerated, without however this description being final and definitive. The general opinion of European law experts here

> is namely that this clause is soft and that new tasks can be subsumed here as far as they do not contradict the general founding principles of the community and serve the day-to-day running of the community and the realization of its goals.

It is interesting to note that the EEC was realized along the schema proposed by Coudenhove-Kalergi in that it came about through three essential unifications, first a governmental summit, second a contract followed by a trade union, followed, third, by the final step yet to be realized, the foundation of the political union that Coudenhove-Kalergi called 'The United States of Europe.'

The integration function of the *European Parliament* became especially important after the first direct election of the parliamentarians in 1979.

This should however not let us forget that the most important lever for European integration is Article 18 EEC Charter that stipulates as the first integrative step the realization of a *trade union with a unified customs index* for all member states of the community.

The second fundamental integrative step then will be the *political union* or foundation of a European Republic through the unification of national political decision-making by the supranational decision-making of the *United States of Europe* that first of all would require a unified foreign politics.

> —Art. 105 EEC Charter only speaks of the 'coordination of the national economic policies.' The political union can thus not be realized under the present conceptual framework of the EEC Charter but needs a fundamental new agreement of all members of the EEC so as to enlarge the competences of the European executive forces and grant them direct executive powers within the territorial sovereignty of each member state.

The Restriction of National Sovereignty

This was the most important point in the proposal of the Belgian prime minister Leo Tindemans in 1975 which consolidated the results of the first official proclamation of the European Union during the Paris Summit in 1972.

> —Bulletin of the European Community (Bull. EC), Addendum 1/1976.

The Integrational Model

It is interesting to note that a unified foreign policy was namely not contained in the union's task catalog proposed by Tindemans, but that only a common attitude of all member states was required in this important point.

> —Paragraph I. B. 1, p. 13 of the Tindemans Memo.

As the reader might remember from my discussion of the historical draft conventions, it is rather the constitutionalists such as Abbé de Saint-Pierre, Rousseau and Kant who require a *strong unified political force* and supranational executive power, whereas the integrationalists, Saint-Simon and Coudenhove-Kalergi, tend to be much more reluctant with conferring executive political powers to the unified political government of the new supranational union.

And when we see that Tindemans was openly on the side of the integrationalists, we might better understand why his draft was lacking out in one of the most important constituents of a true political union: a central government with independent political powers and a strong executive.

In fact, Tindemans wrote the integrational system directly in his report.

—Paragraph I. B. 6, p. 13 of the Tindemans Memo.

After the first direct election of the European Parliament, the *Genscher-Colombo-Plan* presented at the London Summit in 1981 represents a further milestone in the *integrative-pragmatic direction* and focuses on an extension of existing integrative levers, as for example a concerted action between the European Commission and the European Parliament and the revision of certain developments in the aftermath of the *Luxembourg Compromise* of 1966.

> — Bull. EP Nr. 50/1981, p. 31 und EA 1982/2, pp. 50 ff. See also the comment of Pauline Neville-Jones, The Genscher/Colombo Proposals on European Union, in: Common Marked Law Review, Vol. 20 (1983), pp. 657-699. At p. 660 he writes: 'This was destined to be the single most contentious issue which more than anything else held up adoption of the Act by a full year.'

A central point in this plan is the *European Political Cooperation (EPC)* that was elaborated in the Luxembourg Rapport 1970, the Copenhagen Rapport 1973 and the London Rapport 1981.

> — See Eric Stein, The European Community in 1983: A less Perfect Union?, Common Marked Law Review, Vol. 20 (1983), pp. 641-656, 651-652; European Political Cooperation (EPC) as a Component of the European Foreign Affairs System, ZaöRV Vol. 42 (1983), pp. 49 ff. See also See EA 1982/2, pp. 45 ff.

The EPC, which was called in the London Rapport 1981 a *central factor of the member states' foreign policies*, is an obvious parallel to Abbé de Saint-Pierre's idea of a supranational governmental concertation, be it restricted to foreign policy.

That the EPC can be developed into a true political union is subject to doubt, first because it has no normative function, and second because the important sector of a

THE RESTRICTION OF NATIONAL SOVEREIGNTY

common defense policy for the European Union was from the start excluded.

> —See Eric Stein, The European Community in 1983 (1983), 651: 'E.P.C. is not a part of the community system, but it is closely linked to it through what one might call, a 'personal union.' The E.P.C. has no normative foundation.' See also Paragraph I. B. 1, p. 13 of the Tindemans Memo.

A political will to extend the range of what might be called high-level political partying is certainly not enough to bring about what is the most badly needed in present-day Europe: *a common defense strategy* and a concisely elaborated, unified foreign policy.

To repeat it, the invasion of Iraq showed where we are heading if Europe is *not to become a true political union* that forms an important democratic power block in 21st century world politics.

The Constitutional Model

Already during the foundation of the Montan Union, 1951-1952 there were negotiations for a later *European Defense Community (EDC)* and in that draft convention was foreseen that the Congress of that organization was given the competence for drafting a first *European Constitution*.

In an ad-hoc meeting a first draft for such a constitution was elaborated. However, as the EDC failed to be ratified by the French parliament, a unification of the national defense policies became obsolete.

A later attempt to unify national defense strategies contained in the so-called *Fouchet-Plans (1963)* failed as well, perhaps because of lacking vision regarding the need to elaborate a common defense policy.

But we still face a much more general question, which is, how to build a true

THE RESTRICTION OF NATIONAL SOVEREIGNTY

European Union as a politically functional organism, and doing this without incorporating the unification of internal, external and defense politics?

I think it must estrange any honest fighter for the European cause that unfortunately none of these crucial concerns was contained in the *Foundation of a European Union of February 14, 1984.*

> —See EA 1984, pp. 209 ff.

While in Part Four of the chart, an independent economic policy of the union is announced, none of the subsequent articles, especially Article 47, contains detailed provisions to this effect. What this draft thus represents is a *blank paper convention* with nothing to even slightly modify the status quo.

Instead of a common foreign policy, Article 64 enumerates as 'common action areas' only domains that anyway are within the competence of the EEC. Instead of a unified defense policy, Article 68 only contains a chewing-gum provision that says that 'the European Council can extent common action also for questions of foreign policy.'

A European Constitution?

We can thus conclude that historically two different models have been drafted that were elaborated for bringing about a European Union or European Republic, a *constitutional model* and an *integrational model*.

The *constitutional model* foresaw the creation of a *European Constitution* through some sort of concerted, unified and legislative action of the European sovereigns that resulted in a supranational government (Abbé de Saint-Pierre, Rousseau, Kant) or a *European Parliament* (Saint-Simon),

THE RESTRICTION OF NATIONAL SOVEREIGNTY

conceding *independence and sovereignty* to this new organization in the general interest of all European member states and under the restriction of national interests.

The integrational model projects a federal Europe being brought about through a dynamic, phased process from a pan-European conference until the final step of a *pan-European republic*. This model, as I mentioned already, was elaborated by Count Coudenhove-Kalergi, while the idea was already present with Count Saint-Simon.

In all peace proposals, a parliamentarian and republican political system was seen as an important 'in-group landmark' and condition for preparing the 'out-group achievement' of a supranational confederation in which all member states would *restrict their sovereignty* to a certain extent so as to grant independence and sovereignty to the new confederative legal and administrative body.

This idea is of such high impact that it goes like a red thread through all European politics until this very day. In fact, all present-day European integration projects are to be retraced to this tradition and historical parallel.

European law experts agree about Article 237 of the EEC Charter containing an *unwritten condition* for the admission of new members: they must comply with the requirement of a *parliamentary democratic constitutional system* that however can also be formed as a constitutional monarchy.

>   —See Werner Meng in: Groeben/Boeckh/Thiesing/Ehlermann, Kommentar zum EWG-Vertrag (1983), §237, 23.

As a matter of fact, Article 2 of the *Draft Convention of the European Parliament for a*

THE RESTRICTION OF NATIONAL SOVEREIGNTY

European Political Union requires more than Article 237 of the EEC contract in that only a 'democratic European state' can apply for membership in the union. The discussion goes until our very days what the *precise requirements* are of that unwritten republican clause and they have been a part of the heated public debate about Turkey's anticipated membership.

> —See Meinhard Hilf, Die rechtliche Bedeutung des Verfassungsprinzips der parlamentarischen Demokratie für den europäischen Integrationsprozess, EuR 1984, p. 9 ff.

This principle is valid as an unwritten addendum to Article 237 EEC contract. As Nicolaysen pointed out:

> Doubts are not possible regarding the founding principles of the union's constitution: they can in Western Europe only be based upon democratic and civil rights; in addition, this constitution can in fact only be a republican one.

THE UNITED STATES OF EUROPE

> —Gert Nicolaysen, Vom Beruf zur Verfassunggebung in Europa—Fragestellungen zu einem Thema, EuR 1984, pp. 94-97, at 96. (Translation mine)

When we look at the present-day attempts to bring about a European Union through drafting a *European Constitution*, and compare these endeavors with the historical projects for bringing about peace and stability in Europe, we quickly recognize that we are looking in a simulation cabinet. What is presented with lots of pomp, glamour, power display and media coverage is in fact blindfolding the masses about a political reality in today's Europe I would qualify as 'stagnation' because the integrational dynamics appear to be regressing below a standard we have achieved about fifteen years ago.

I have tried to show that drafts and papers to bring about a true political union have

THE RESTRICTION OF NATIONAL SOVEREIGNTY

deceived the public point by point since the *Luxembourg Compromise* of 1966 in that they did not contain one single of the founding constitutional elements we have seen present in all historical convention drafts.

To speak of a real European Union, simply because the original EEC now has not only six, but more than forty members, is another way to blindfold the media-hypnotized masses about the fact that surely in a sandbox of forty, litigations are going to be much more difficult, and not easier, to realize than in a sandbox of six. And to even dream of ideas being realized in a gigantic Europe of forty which were not realized in an initial Europe of six borders journalistic and political eye-wiping. From this perspective, it looks rather as Utopia than future reality to consider 'The United States of Europe' as a full political union being realized anywhere in the near future.

As a matter of fact, and as a bitter note to conclude this article, the only thing that was realized without problem for the greater Europe was the following:

- The creation of a supranational European police force called EUROPOL;

- Concerted action of all members to increasingly spy out and control citizens by lowering civil rights and constitutional guarantees;

- Concerted action of all members to create a common ID card for all European citizens that allows police and paramilitary forces to control and persecute individuals beyond national borders.

Nothing, by contrast, was foreseen and agreed upon that enlarges or safeguards civil rights and guarantees for new member states; the only advantages, then, it seems, for new members to join the union are of a mere financial nature. No big deal after so much ado about nothing!

THE RESTRICTION OF NATIONAL SOVEREIGNTY

However, the European law expert will not for that matter give up being positive about a final success of the European unification idea; what was eye-wiping has been recognized as such; the intelligent, educated and critical European citizen intuitively knows that the media images cannot be trusted.

Beyond the perspective one can gain from politics, with all its absurdities, the expert knows that the real progress of the European idea was largely the long-term insistence upon *integration*, as an incremental and step-by-step process.

Personally, I am a believer in the *integration idea* because I have known the details and studied and practiced European law for a good time.

My mistrust in the constitutionalist idea is because the door is wide open, with that kind of idea, for political cunningness, media manipulation and lobbyism until outright media bluff. Nothing in our world that involves large masses of people and a change of the political landscape is created overnight, by publishing a decorated 'Constitution' that propagates the best for all, in no time, and for no price to pay, like the proverbial *manna* falling from heaven.

This is something good for the rainbow press, but not for those who, like myself, know the intricate details of the process. To say, the European idea is not dead, it's still very much alive, but it's better put in the hands of the generally invisible crowd of legal experts, advisors, administrators, and judges than in the white gloves of our glamorous politicians and their blind followers.

On the surface level, Europe 2020 will probably not be much different from Europe 2015, and for insiders and academia this is not something to regret. The transitions we are living through in this moment and over the next twenty years are of such a grandeur, of such a revolutionary impact, and of such a daringness that we cannot reasonably expect them to happen overnight, nor to be effected and carried out without hurt or sacrifices.

On the surface, changes seem to be nonexistent when in reality the time factor is such that slowness makes for steadiness; behind the veil of public appearance, where change is incremental and slow, true progress is being made.

This slowness of progress is not a bad thing to happen, by the way. All solid progress is slow, look only at plants, not to talk about the time from the big bang until today or the time our human race needed to emerge on the globe. When you look at a plant or a tree, you get the feeling that nothing is growing, or changing, and this is, as we all know, a wrong perception. When you see a tree that is a few hundred years old or a giant tortoise whose age can be up to three thousand years, you get an idea of the fact that time is relative and that for trees and giant tortoises, time is certainly different than for humans.

How can we predict how much time 'it should take' to transform a world of unfreedom, violence and rampant injustice into a world of freedom, of peace, of justice and of respect for all sentient beings?

All religions have speculated about this important question, but at the end, when you have studied all this, and look at the present world, you become rather down-to-earth in your approach and you feel that such speculations really lead nowhere. What however contributes to change, and what progresses the change agenda, is positive

THE RESTRICTION OF NATIONAL SOVEREIGNTY

thinking and consistency in upholding a vision and the values connected to it!

Many intelligent world citizens today have this vision and are lucidly aware of the necessary values behind this vision, and there is consensus about the core values of a functional and smooth society that is able to be of assistance to human progress, instead of opposing human progress.

These values are obvious, they are so basic as values can be basic; we live in a world that is upside-down in every respect: there is war, strife, hunger, violence, and oppression, globally, and all this is not normal, and not in the genetic program of the human race.

To bring about peace, we need to focus on the *simple human values* that virtually every child knows and instinctively follows, and which are love, respect, freedom, understanding of our needs, and help and support for those in growth, and those in need, and this without regard to race, ethnic belonging, culture, family background, or language.

All problems can be solved, provided there is a will, but this will is lacking in our present societies because the political priority is not problem-solving but *problem administration*.

There are many people, among them many politicians, who earn more money with *administrating our worldwide problems* than they would earn by solving them.

Our endeavor for transforming present society is motivated and fueled by the idea of establishing a *world government* as the *safer solution* compared to a bunch of highly armed nation states who share in a scarcity paradigm, fighting for 'survival resources,' thus jeopardizing world peace, and who, by their endless insistence on 'national values,' in truth

THE RESTRICTION OF NATIONAL SOVEREIGNTY

defy human values. The struggle for 'quick solutions' loses its attractiveness when you consider the bigger agenda and its ultimate purpose, *world peace.*

And applying the wisdom of the Book of Changes, the I Ching, we know that hastening growth regularly 'destroys the fruit.' Timeless wisdom and the observation of living systems coincide in affirming that every true and solid growth needs time, and that often, with larger projects, the time needed is very difficult to predict in advance.

The model, if ever, for building a united world, is not the United States but will be the *United States of Europe*, once they are realized. And this for very tangible reasons.

The United States of America, at the time of their creation were a *quite homogenous structure* compared to Europe, which is rather heterogenous. In addition, psychologically, the United States were *new land*, and the settlers were in quite the same situation, facing novelty, and thereby forming a common purpose, in alignment with their very similar needs and visions.

In Europe, every country has a different history and a still more strikingly different culture.

To look at the three 'classical' examples, to show their essential difference in lifestyle, take Germany, France and Italy. Three countries, so different in cultural background, lifestyle and personal habits, so different in the culinary sector, so different in spending habits, so different in marriage and family attitudes and the education of children, and then you want to bring them under one hat, and let one government decide about their future?!

It's really an idea hostile to most European nationals, in their quality as nationals, in their role as Germans, French and Italians, while a lesser hostile idea in their role as Europeans.

And it's exactly to what extent they accept their fresh 'European' identity that the whole idea is going to work, or is *not* going to work in the long run. And it's for that and other reasons that the testing arena for a possible world unification is not the USA but the USE, namely when we have mastered the challenge to get to look over our national fences, as these fences used to be high and opaque.

BIBLIOGRAPHY

Contextual Bibliography

ADEDE, A.D.

The United Kingdom Abandons the Doctrine of Absolute Sovereign Immunity
6 BROOKLYN J. INT'L L. 1997-215 (1980)

AGUDA, AKINOLA

Law and Practice Relating to Evidence in Nigeria
LONDON: SWEET & MAXWELL, 1980

AMERICAN LAW INSTITUTE

Model Code on Evidence
CHESTNUT, PHILADELPHIA, 1942

AUSTRALIA

The Law Reform Commission
REFORM OF EVIDENCE LAW 1980

Discussion Paper N° 16
Canberra: Australian Government Publishing Service, 1980

Bennion, Francis

Statutory Interpretation
London: Butterworths, 1984

Cairns, Bernard C.

Australian Civil Procedure
Sydney: The Law Book Company Ltd., 1981

Canada

Uniform Evidence Act, Livre II
Règles Générales de Preuve, Titre I, Fardeau de la Preuve

Report of the Federal/Provincial Task Force on Uniform Rules of Evidence
Prepared for the Uniform Law Conference of Canada
Toronto: The Carswell Company Ltd., 1982 [U.L.C.C. Report]

Coyne, Thomas A.

Rules of Civil Procedure for the United States District Courts
Practice Comments
New York: Clark Boardman Company Ltd., 1983

Cross, Sir Rupert

Cross on Evidence
5th ed.
London: Butterworths, 1979

Cross on Evidence
2nd Australian Edition
By J.A. Gobbo, David Byrne, J.D. Heydon
Sidney: Butterworths, 1980

Cross, Sir Rupert & Wilkins, Nancy

An Outline of the Law of Evidence
5th Edition
London: Butterworths, 1980

Curzon, L.B.

Law of Evidence
Plymouth: McDonald & Evans Ltd., 1978

Eggleston, Sir Richard

Evidence, Proof and Probability
2nd Edition
London: Weidenfels & Nicholson, 1983

Glasbeek, Harry J.

Evidence Cases and Materials
Toronto: Butterworths, 1977

Cases and Materials on Evidence
Australian Edition
Sydney: Butterworths, 1974

Graham, Michael H.

Evidence
Text, Rules, Illustrations and Problems
The Commentary Method
St. Paul (Minn.): National Institute for Trial Advocacy, 1983

Federal Rules of Evidence in a Nutshell
St. Paul (Minn.): American Textbook Series, 1981

Harvard University

A Uniform System of Citation
13th Edition

CAMBRIDGE, MASS.: HARVARD LAW REVIEW ASSOCIATION, 1982

HOFFMANN & ZEFFERT

South African Law of Evidence
3RD EDITION
DURBAN: BUTTERWORTHS, 1983

JAMES, FLEMING & HAZARD, GEOFFREY

Civil Procedure
2ND EDITION

JOWITT'S DICTIONARY OF ENGLISH LAW

2nd Edition, by John Burke
LONDON: SWEET & MAXWELL, 1977

LAL, JADGISH

Code of Civil Procedure, 1908
AS AMENDED UP TO DATE BY C.P.C. AMENDMENT ACT N° 104 OF 1976
ALLAHABAD: LAW PUBLISHERS SARDAR PATEL, 1981

Lilly, Graham C.

An Introduction to the Law of Evidence
St. Paul (West), 1978

Maxwell on the Interpretation of Statutes

12th ed., by P. St. J. Langan
London: Sweet & Maxwell, 1969

McCormick

McCormick on Evidence
by Edward W. Cleary, 3d ed.
Lawyers Edition (Homebook Series)
St. Paul: West, 1984

Moore, James W.

Moore's Federal Practice
2nd Edition, 1979

Nash, Gerard

Civil Procedure
Cases and Text
Sydney: The Law Book Company Ltd., 1976

Ninth Decennial Digest

American Digest System
PART I, 1976-1981

Phipson

Phipson on Evidence
13TH ED., BY JOHN HUXLEY BUZZARD
RICHARD MAY AND M. N. HOWARD
LONDON: SWEET & MAXWELL, 1982

Phipson and Elliott

Manual of the Law of Evidence
11TH EDITION
BY D. W. ELLIOTT
LONDON: SWEET & MAXWELL, 1980

Rothstein, Paul F.

Evidence in a Nutshell: State and Federal Rules
2ND EDITION
ST. PAUL (WEST), 1981

Row, Sanjiva

Code of Civil Procedure (Act V of 1908)
BY MALIK
3RD EDITION, VOL. 1
ALLAHABAD: LAW BOOK COMPANY, 1962

Rules of Civil Procedure for the United States District Courts

Practice Comments by Thomas A. Coyne
NEW YORK: CLARK BOARDMAN COMPANY LTD., 1983

Sarkar's Law of Evidence

India, Pakistan, Bangladesh, Burma & Ceylon
13TH EDITION
BY PRABHAS C. SARKAR AND SUDIPTO SARKAR
CALCUTTA: S. C. SARKAR & SONS, 1981

Sarkar on Civil Procedure

6th Edition, as amended by Act 104 of 1976
BY PRABHAS C. SARKAR AND SUDIPTO SARKAR
CALCUTTA: S. C. SARKAR & SONS, 1979

Smith, P. F. / Bailey, S.

The Modern English Legal System
London: Sweet & Maxwell, 1984

Sutherland

Statutory Construction
Ed. By Sands
4th Edition
London, 1975

Tayer, James Bradley

A Preliminary Treatise on Evidence
1898

The English and Empire Digest

Vol. 22, 'Evidence'
London: Butterworths, 1974

Walker & Walker

The English Legal System
6th Edition, by R.J. Walker
London: Butterworths, 1985

WIGMORE, JOHN HENRY

A Treatise on the Anglo-American System of Evidence in Trials at Common Law
10 VOLUMES, VOL. 9 'EVIDENCE IN TRIALS AT COMMON LAW'
REV. BY JAMES H. CHADBURN
BOSTON, TORONTO: LITTLE, BROWN & COMPANY, 1981

WOODROFFE & AMER ALI

Law of Evidence
14TH EDITION
ED. AND REV. BY B. R. P. SINGHAL AND NARAYAN DAS
ALLAHABAD: LAW BOOK COMPANY LTD., 1979

WORDS AND PHRASES LEGALLY DEFINED

Ed. by John B. Saunders
2ND EDITION
LONDON: BUTTERWORTHS, 1969

WRIGHT, MILLER & COOPER

Federal Practice and Procedure, 1975

Personal Notes